S

I0983522

"EBY"

Master of the Moment

BY

BURT HERMAN

the Peppertree Press
Sarasota, Florida

3 1969 02637 3851

Until I discovered them decades later, my hero
pilot and fellow passengers were lost in the fourth
dimension as we each journeyed along our individual
landscapes unaware of the other.

Gratitude

High altitude gratitude to reporters Tony Holt, Wayne Grant, Anna Brugmann, Chuck Fieldman, David Tucker, and other members of the fourth estate in Florida and Chicago who helped me bring attention to this story.

Thanks to Guy Eby's sons, Wayne and Robert, for sharing some great stories about their dad, to Guy's step-daughters, Penney and Paula Peirce, and step-granddaughter, Julia Proschaka, for their insights. Much appreciation to my daughter, Leslie, for helping me organize my material and special thanks to 182 passengers, Mary Florence, Marla, Hal, Kathleen, Mary Beth, Elaine, Larry, Laura, and Leslie, for their stirring "voices."

And my undying gratitude to our pilot, Guy Eby, "The Master of the Moment," whose training, experience, and instincts saved me and my family and hundreds of others aboard two jumbo jets from almost certain death, some 37,000 feet above Carleton, Michigan, Thanksgiving eve 1975.

Table of Contents

"An 85-year-old Oak Brook man has taken on the roles of author and investigator to tell the story of a former American Airlines pilot he believes likely saved the lives of himself and his family nearly 42 years ago."

—*Chicago Tribune* 7/7/17

ONE

The Passenger

Thanksgiving Eve, 2017

Chicago, Illinois

I was a passenger on an airplane that nearly blew up in the sky 37,000 feet above Carleton, Michigan, on one of the snowiest Thanksgiving weekends forty-two years ago. My wife, three children, and I and 304 other passengers and crew aboard two jumbo jets didn't die November 26, 1975, because of the instincts and skills of one man.

Captain Guy Eby

TWO

The Pilot

Thanksgiving Eve 1975

The Night Sky above Carleton, Michigan

We came up out of the clouds into the starry night.
What was Guy Eby's state of mind when he saw the bright stars against the black sky in a break in the dense clouds? Was he reminded as I was of pictures of night skies in children's books that I once pored over? Or reminded of a dream he once had that he could fly, a dream of sailing barely above the still black water of a lake in late summer with the wind in his face and tickling his fingers and toes. Did the blackness of the night sky and the brightness of the stars in the blackness thrill him?

Inexplicably a glow lit up the clouds beyond Guy's windscreen and he knew instantly what was out there. He plunged the yoke of the DC-10 violently forward, sending the plane into a sudden nosedive.

THREE

Early Years

1926

Hershey, Pennsylvania

Guy Eby glanced down at the landing in the center hall below. The morning sunlight on the hardwood floor made the floorboards appear white. His hightop gym shoes made almost no sound as he descended the stairs, heading to the kitchen for breakfast. Guy's bedroom on the second story of the clapboard and brick house had a view of the front yard and across Areba Street to an identical Hershey house. In the town of Hershey, Pennsylvania, many houses were designed and built by Hershey, as well as public buildings with the Hershey name on them.

Guy had breakfast alone with his mother, since his father left early for work at the hardware store. What Guy lacked in not having a brother or sister, he made up for in friends. The eight-year-old was a happy-go-lucky kid to whom children and adults were drawn.

This morning at Guy's place at the kitchen table, resting

on two small rubber wheels was a replica of the "Spirit of St. Louis," which his father had made for him for his birthday. His father had set the toy plane on the table before he left for work, knowing that the hour it would be discovered by his son, the angle of the sun would reach the silver fuselage and make it shine as brightly as the square on the hall floorboards.

The "Spirit of St. Louis" went with Guy to school two blocks away. It was a cool November morning, but the sun on the back of Guy's neck felt hot as he walked with his head bent searching the sidewalk for treasures. Though he was thrilled by the feel of the small plane in his right hand, his attention was on something glittering in the sunlight on the street as he entered the first of two alley shortcuts to his school. The shiny object was a chain of some sort.

He reached down to the gray cement for the silver-colored chain that had dirt imbedded in the links and studied the machine work of the links before dropping the chain in his pants pocket. Guy knew it was not a bicycle chain, because he had a bike, one of two bicycles among his friends. His bike, a hand-me-down from his father's brother, was too large for him, but Guy had taught himself to stretch for the pedals without losing his balance. Guy's best friend, Clyde, who lived on the other side of town, owned the other bike.

Guy spent nearly as much time that day in school, turning the chain over in his hands and puzzling over it, as he did admiring each detail of the plane his father had made for him. He knew if he couldn't figure out the chain's purpose by dinner time, his father would know. At eight years old, Guy was curious about everything under the sun, especially how things worked. Everything in the hardware store his father managed had a purpose and he wanted to know that purpose.

On his way home from school that day, Guy slipped between two black Ford sedans parked on the street, one with a for sale sign attached to the rear window. The eight-year-old took a quick glance down the street for any horse-drawn carts and the occasional Model T, saw none, and skipped across the street, deciding the chain he'd found had broken off a conveyor of some sort, because its links, like a bicycle chain, looked meant to engage the points of a wheel of some sort.

Arriving home hours before his father returned from work, Guy had plenty of time to collect the cooled ashes from the furnace and take them to the curb.

As he came out of the second alley, nearly home, he imagined what was taking place in his backyard. Chummy wasn't able to see him yet, but his dog always sensed when Guy was on his way home to him, stood up on his four legs, and wagged his tail in anticipation. The cocker-spaniel's tail wagged so strongly when he heard Guy whistle that the dog lost his balance and fell over onto his back on the cold November ground.

The boy laughed at the sight as he came around the house across the straw-colored lawn. Guy had a husky laugh for his eight years and slight frame. It sounded like rocks rolling around in a barrel and amused his friends and his mother from whom he had inherited his sense of humor. He would never be as tall or as muscular as his friend, Clyde, who had large feet and meaty hands, but Guy was fast on his feet and coordinated. He could scale the fence between his house and his neighbor's without much effort and that pleased him.

Guy's only enemy, Ralph, was the school bully, who followed him on the playground at school, mocking him for no reason other than that's what Ralph did—he mimicked the young kids until they cried. Guy wasn't afraid and a better wrestler than anyone would expect. One day he put a move on Ralph, came in low, and pulled the bully's legs out from under him. Those who had witnessed the take-down saw Guy smile as he walked away.

From a hook in the ceiling over his bed, Guy hung the "Spirit of St. Louis." In his imagination he was in the cockpit, looking down at himself in bed.

FOUR

Early Signs

1930

Hershey, Pennsylvania

It was raining hard by the time Guy reached the alley a block from his house. He pulled up the collar of his jacket and turned into the second alley, then skidded across the street, his shoes slapping the water in his path. He ran into the school through the boiler room on the ground floor, rather than up the concrete steps to the front door of the middle school. Guy said he never encountered classmates in the boiler room on rainy days or on the spiral staircase he took up to his classroom on the first floor, and he never questioned that or questioned himself for taking that route. "It was the quickest way out of the rain," he said. "It made sense." He wasn't troubled by not following the crowd, nor did he invite anyone to go his way.

Hours later, on the third story of a friend's house, Guy was studying the engine on Dick's train set.

"Can you see what's wrong?" Dick asked, expecting a yes or a nod from Guy who was smiling. The two friends were huddled together at the table in the large room that was devoted entirely to the elaborate train track.

"Yeah, it's not this," Guy answered, and he picked up the train's transformer and pointed to a wire that exited it. "This must have separated from the rail when the engine came round that last curve." Guy was leaning over the table, holding up a piece of track now. The two friends spent most of their afternoons after school playing with the old train set, working on its track, moving the model buildings and turf and trees around, and sitting, staring at the line of cars pulled by the engine around bends, over hills, and under bridges.

The electric train was all Guy and Dick were interested in and, for Guy in particular, the wires that fed electricity to it. The two boys had been in school together since kindergarten at the Milton Hershey Consolidated School that sat on 486 acres and had an elementary, middle, and high school, as well as a vocational school on that location. Guy would later study electronics, physics, and math at the vocational school.

Guy had a second close friend that he went through middle school with and beyond. Clyde lived on the other side of town, where the fathers were all blue collar workers and the houses were modest. Guy spent his teenage years and nearly every weekend in Clyde's garage, working on one jalopy after another and every Thursday night in the pool at the Community Club that was endowed by the Hershey family.

The Community Club was an impressive building that looked more like Faneuil Hall in Boston than a community club and housed a gym, pool hall, bowling alley, and ping pong room, in addition to an Olympic-sized swimming pool. The entire building smelled like teenage boys—not even the swimming pool's chlorine could mask the smell of body odor coming off Hershey's young population.

"Race you to the shallow end," Clyde said.

"Race you there and back," Guy challenged.

The two counted down from five to one and dove in. Guy's body, slim and strong, cut through the water like a shark, while husky Clyde fought like a dog to get to the surface and begin his stroke. On the turn at the deep end of the pool, Guy pushed off the blue-tiled wall and glided underwater as long as he could, because he knew though it didn't look like a faster way, it was. The swimmer with the least resistance won the race. Guy won a lot of races, but Clyde never tired of challenging him at swimming and skating, target practice, and throwing darts.

Guy had two Uncle Henrys. The older was Guy's great-uncle, his mother's first uncle. The younger was his mother's brother.

Great-Uncle Henry had a circular saw blade that was three feet across, hanging on a wall in his basement.

"You'll know by the sound, if you hit the bull's eye," Uncle Henry said to Clyde who was there with Guy and new to the sport. Clyde lined up the sight on the hole in the center of the saw blade. "It will clonk, if you miss the hole and hit the saw and clink if you hit bull's eye," Guy told him

"Clonk, clonk, clonk!"

Guy laughed.

"I've got it," Clyde said. Then, "Clonk, clonk, clonk!" Guy restrained himself and didn't laugh, but Clyde knew his friend was laughing on the inside. "Oh, go ahead and show me how to do it," Clyde said, handing over the gun to Guy.

Guy lined up the sight and, "Clink!"

"You're too damn lucky," Clyde said, but he knew it was more than luck with Guy. Clyde could tolerate losing regularly to Guy, because his friend never laid it on thick. When Guy sent the winning puck into the net at the hockey rink, he looked at Clyde and said, "Just was at the right place at the right time." Guy said that often enough that Clyde thought his friend somehow knew where the right place would be a second before anyone else.

FIVE

At Seventeen

1935

Hershey, Pennsylvania

Guy stood beside the Model T in Clyde's garage with a wrench in his greasy hand. The seventeen-year-old was helping his buddy transform the old car into a tractor by adding a scoop to the front end. The Haybackers didn't own a car so their two-car garage became a body shop for the teenagers. Guy was also working on a four-cylinder Model B coup, but dreaming one day of having a 1935 Ford convertible—a four-door sedan that had a gray body and a tan top.

When Guy wasn't working on cars, he was handing out advertising bills for Hershey Department Store, ushering at the sports arena, or caddying at the Hershey Country Club for 75 cents a round and a 15 to 25 cent tip.

It was the Depression, but folks in Hershey were doing okay, because candy was always in demand. The hardware business was brisk, if low-paying, so Guy's father didn't have to worry about unemployment and Guy's mother played the piano for the silent movies.

At seventeen, Guy was slim enough to slide easily under the body of a Model B. On chilly days, he wore a pair of worn-out corduroys that he used as much as a grease rag as pants. He was perpetual motion, always had a tool in his hand that he gestured with, and often carried the tool away from the work area without thinking.

"Come on back here with my wrench," Clyde shouted when Guy absentmindedly slipped the wrench into his back pocket to free both hands for the bike ride home, although once he got started he could take both hands off the handlebars, and if he didn't have to stop, he could ride all the way home that way. The bike Guy now rode had come from the hardware store his father managed. It sat for sale in the hardware so long its handlebars began to rust, so his father gave in to his son's pleas and bought him the bike.

It was 1935 when Guy got his first rifle. It, too, came from the hardware store his father managed. Father and son often went hunting with the local doctor who had a birddog he called Lindy after Lindberg, the pilot. The dog slept on the doctor's examining table in the home office and more than one patient had refused to get up on the table to be examined.

Great-Uncle Henry was always welcome on the hunting trips, as well as Clyde. The mix of Uncle Henry and the doctor promised there would be some joking or poking fun. When they didn't hunt locally, they would drive over to the woods of south Jersey looking for pheasant.

"That Lindy is more trouble than he's worth," Uncle Henry called out when the dog jumped the gun and scared the pheasants out before the hunters were ready.

"I heard he came free," Guy's father answered seriously.

"That was my point," Uncle Henry said. "The dog's worthless."

Guy smiled, amused by uncle's teasing nature, but also appreciating that his father was a perfect straight man to his uncle. Guy later admitted that the banter on those occasions was more fun than the hunting.

Occasionally someone's gun would jam or fishing line would tangle, and it was Guy who had the patience and focus to fix these things. More than once, Guy purposely jammed his rifle and knotted a fishing line just to see how quickly he could make the repair.

SIX

First Job

1936-1940

Pennsylvania, Maryland, and Puerto Rico

Guy Eby's first job after graduation was as an electrician's helper. He was employed by Hershey Electric for 35 cents an hour, $23.76 a week. When his parents moved to Carlisle, Pennsylvania, Guy got a room at the Community Club in Hershey for a-year-and-a-half before moving to the Harrisburg area, where he joined the electricians' union.

In 1939, at 21 years of age, Guy was employed as a shipyard electrician by Bethlehem Steel at Sparrows Point, Maryland. Originally marshland, Sparrows Point had been home to native American tribes. Mid-20th century, it was the largest steel company in the world. The mill's steel ended up as girders on the Golden Gate Bridge, cables on the George Washington Bridge, and was a vital part of the war production during WWI and then WWII in which Guy Eby flew for the Navy.

Late 1939, Guy left Maryland and went to Borinquen Field, Puerto Rico, as an electrical foreman during the construction of the airbase. It was there that he became interested in aviation.

In June of 1940, the first thing Guy did was visit his parents' home in Carlisle on the corner of Louther and North Streets in Carlisle, Pennsylvania. Across North Street from the Eby house sat a brick post office where a large six-foot tall navy poster caught Guy Eby's eye. It pictured a pilot and recruit standing below the huge engine of a navy plane and its giant propellers. The copy on the poster read, "She's all yours when you win your wings of gold."

Guy enlisted in the Naval Aviation Cadet V5 program the following day.

Naval Air Force recuitment poster

SEVEN

The Navy

1943

Chapel Hill, North Carolina

There was a pre-physical for the enlistees at the post office. Men of every size and shape stood in line on the sidewalk in the heat, drinking Cokes, smoking Lucky Strikes, and teasing one another. "Tag, you better get your mother down here with some of her cream pie for Pete 'fore he faints or is blown away by this sea breeze that ain't." And, "Bobby, you can forget about flying. They don't make cockpits large enough for your donkey ass." And, "Guy, we know you're just looking to trade in those high waters for something the ladies like." By evening every last one of them was being sent to Philadelphia headquarters for a thorough exam and blood test. "The only one I saw 'em pass up," Guy began, "had just one leg."

"Nah," Everett answered, "I saw that guy board the first bus."

The morning of the blood test, Guy had a big breakfast of pancakes and his blood sugar level was so high he had to take the test a second time before they would assign him the title, Aviation Cadet.

After a long train ride from Philadelphia, the cadets took a bus from Greensboro, North Carolina, to Chapel Hill, the site of the University of North Carolina, one of several locations for Naval Cadet Preflight Training.

The roadway into the dormitory area was lined with uniformed cadets, welcoming the bus from Greensboro with the chant, "You'll be sorry!" as the dusty bus slowly made its way past them to stop at the boxing rings where eager young men were trying to knock their brains out. Here the new cadets exchanged their civilian clothes for marine khakis, high shoes and athletic gear. Delahanty, Everett, Lasher, and Eby were assigned a room in Grimes Dormitory which had two double overhead bunks. It was the 15th of March 1943. Guy Eby was 25 years old.

On March 16th, Guy was awakened at 5:30 a.m. by the sound of an amplified phonograph over the PA system. The scratching of a needle on a record was followed by the sound of a bugle and the four roommates were up and at 'em to make formation at their assigned company location along the roadway to the boxing rings. During formation and to chow where all battalions were seated together, the station band played marches.

Ground school classes were in math, code recognition, and navy regulations. Sport activity changed each week and in addition to boxing, included gymnastics, football, softball, soccer, swimming, wrestling, and push-ball, the only sport Guy had never played.

It took place on the football field where the object was to roll an eight-foot ball that weighed 75 pounds through the goal posts for a point. Half of each team was on either side of the ball, trying to push it through the goal posts. The other half of the team tried to remove the players in the ball's path. Once a team was able to move the ball with a little speed, it was impossible to stop it. The ball would throw the opposition to the ground and bounce over them on its way to the goal. Push-ball had more injuries than any sport.

The last period of the day was elective sport and Guy chose wrestling though he hadn't wrestled since elementary school when he took down the class bully. Everyone was required to pass the swimming test, non-swimmers included. The requirements were to stay afloat for an hour, swim the length of the pool under water as well as the required number of laps, and learn rescue techniques. Additionally, the cadets had to run an obstacle course in the required time and a half-mile in three minutes.

Liberty was granted every other weekend, but downtown Chapel Hill was just two blocks of small stores, lined with cadets and college students. The few coeds there were, were already attached.

One weekend the roommates rented bicycles and biked over to Duke University. The remaining weekends they stayed put on campus, which spoke to the unspoken, that Duke coeds were a disappointment. Three weeks after their arrival on base, a bus of new cadets arrived with the famous baseball player, Ted Williams. It was then Delahanty, Everett, Lasher, and Eby's turn to line the roadway and cry out, "You'll be sorry."

At the end of training, all cadets were tested for their physical endurance. The most grueling test was the pack test. A sand bag at half the cadet's weight was strapped on his back and the cadet had to hop up and down a twelve-inch step for five minutes and have his pulse and blood pressure checked. Those who could complete the test were sent to Air Corps Language Primary Flight Training and issued gear that included a white officer's uniform with a single star on the shoulder pad.

Guy in uniform

EIGHT

Training

1943

Washington, DC and Dallas, Texas

The graduating cadets could choose their base of training and Bert, Everett, and Guy Eby chose Anacostia. Not the least of considerations was the great liberty town at their doorstep—Washington was across the Anacostia River.

Their first morning a cattle-car tractor-trailer with high open sides and bench seats picked up the cadets. It was not a smooth ride and each time the tractor-trailer hit a bump or took a turn, Guy nearly slid off the bench seat.

"What's the matter, Eby," Bert teased, "You don't have enough meat on that lame ass to hold yourself down?"

Guy stood, spit on the bench, and sat down on his spit to howls of laughter from the row of cadets.

A big palooka of a guy said, "That's some spit." He stood, spat on his seat on the bench, and sat down. One by one they each stood and spat on the bench and sat back down.

"That must be something they taught you all when I was snoozing," Bert said.

They arrived at Hyde Field fifteen miles from the Naval Air Station with their tires kicking up dust as the tractor-trailer came to a halt. When the dust settled, the boys saw about 200 yellow Streamers, biplanes used as military training aircraft, parked on the tarmac. "The airfield was like a giant flag, the formation was so tight and the pattern so geometric," Guy wrote home.

The third day of flight training, Guy told Bert he'd heard they were closing down primary flight training at Hyde Field. Bert was sure Guy was pulling his leg, since the two rarely reported anything honestly to each other. But the rumor was real and Bert and Guy and the others were given leave until orders for transfer to a new airfield came in.

Bert and Guy went to a big mixer on Fourteenth Street. Guy kept a log of his time in training and described their night.

We felt lucky stepping into the club crowded with more women than men. Bert whistled and led the way to the bar. "If you had another foot on you," I said, "you'd be feasting your eyes on the two tens I'm looking at." The tens I was referring to were two beautiful babes with long legs and small waists. It was customary for us to assign numbers to women when we were talking among ourselves and we were careful not to be overheard by any women. I was overheard once and the offended woman berated me, while the men standing around me laughed.

I explained to the lady that I wasn't being disrespectful—I just had a small vocabulary. She didn't let up on me and the guys loved that, so when she asked me, "And what number are you?" the guys howled and wouldn't let up on me. I couldn't do anything but join them in their fun. I said, "That would be a double 0 as in fool."

Bert grabbed two beers off the bar and weaved his way through the crowd in the direction I had indicated. He was expecting a couple of "twos," but this time I had told him the truth and Bert returned to the bar with the two lovely women in tow. One had long flaxen hair and round blue eyes and the other was dark and simmered under her black cropped bob and full lips. Bert and I were giddy in their presence. After an evening of drinks with the two women, we saw them home in a cab. All four of us sat in the back seat of the cab with the women sitting on our laps. Back at the barracks, Bert and I discovered our white pants were streaked with tan leg makeup. The next night was a repeat performance—more tan leg makeup on our only change of clean, white pants. The next day, I slipped into an empty classroom and lifted a piece of chalk from the blackboard as a temporary fix.

Orders came in the following day and Bert and Guy were given 48 hours liberty. Guy had to decide whether to go to Carlisle, Pennsylvania, to visit his folks and have a possible date with an old girlfriend or stay in Washington with Janet from the last two nights. He stayed until dawn with Janet, caught a train to Harrisburg when the sun came up, and a bus from there to Carlisle, arriving with two white uniforms caked with chalk and ground-in dirt. During his short visit home, his mother laundered his uniforms without saying a word.

The Chapel Hill 22nd Battalion cadets arrived at their new air station to continue training midway between Dallas and Fort Worth. Quarters, ground school, and athletic activity were conducted at the Naval Air Station in Dallas and flying at Grand Prairie.

The base had army-type barracks painted white, a large drill hall, classrooms, swimming pool, and obstacle course.

Ground school was conducted afternoons with classes in navigation, meteorology, engine operation, and sports including swimming. Navigation included use of a computer that could plot the pilot's course, heading, drift, ground speed, true air speed, relative motion intercepts, sector, square, relative searches, and maintain the pilot's position.

The morning of July 9th, Guy's group boarded a cattle car for Grand Prairie where four hundred N2S aircraft were on the flight line.

Guy wrote:

The field had two mats that were hexagon-shaped and about two thousand feet in diameter—one was used for takeoff and the other for landing. In the hangar, there were several blackboards listing the plane numbers, instructor's name, cadet's name, and type of flight.

"The weather is good for flying," the officer with the Texas accent said. "All flights will take off when scheduled."

I checked out my instructor's chute and one for myself and met Ensign Lewis from a cattle ranch in Florida. We walked to the plane.

My first flight was a familiarization of the area and the outlying fields: Arlington, Cedar Hill, Duncanville, and Manchester. There were two pylons two thousand feet apart about two miles from the mats at Grand Prairie and a single pylon another mile from the field. Returning to base, we flew between the first two and then across the single pylon. Later we understood that this was basic formation flying.

Our first stage in training included take-off and landings, stalls, spins, dragging the field, emergency landings, high-altitude emergencies and S-turning to touch down in a hundred feet circle. We were required to complete three out of six good landings in order to advance.

My instructor, Ensign Lewis seated himself in the front seat of our assigned plane and handed down to me on the tarmac the crank handle to insert into the engine's starter. I cranked the geared internal flywheel until it produced a high whine, which took a considerable amount of energy, then removed the crank handle and pulled the tee handle that engaged the starter. The starter had enough energy to turn the engine about six revolutions, but the engine fired on the first try.

While the engine idled, I climbed into the rear seat and connected the Gosport hose to my helmet. The Gosport is a one-way communication system that allowed Ensign Lewis to speak to me. At times, it was difficult to understand him and we used hand signals—tapping the top of my head meant I had control of the aircraft. Lewis shook the stick to tell me he was taking control. A mirror attached to the upper wing enabled us to see each other, and for Lewis to see me shake my head yes or no. Lewis became an excellent lip reader.

We spent free time at the field in the code room until we could receive twelve words a minute to pass code. No code, no liberty, which was granted every other weekend.

On our first liberty, Bert, Bill Springman, Walter Eichelberger, and I discovered Dallas. After walking Elm, Main, and Commerce, we entered the bar at the street-level entrance in the Adolphus Hotel, named after the Baron Aldophus Busch and said to be the most beautiful building west of Venice. It was a 22-floor baroque structure with gold leaf on the walls and in the fabric decorations.

Bill and Walt left Bert and me at the oak bar that seated about thirty patrons. Peggy, the bartender, was a good-looking barkeep with auburn hair and a friendly manner. It was pleasant enough watching her serve drinks and chatting with the patrons. An added bonus for me arrived at the bar, seated herself next to me, and ordered a drink. She was not only a looker, but congenial. After several drinks, she told me her name was Mary Elizabeth. She was the general's secretary at Love Field and lived in the Adolphus Hotel. I stayed at the bar with Mary Elizabeth for three more hours.

The second stage in our training included acrobatics. The instructors demonstrated a maneuver, and then it was our turn to do the same. The required maneuvers consisted of the bird cage, split-five loop followed by snap rolls, slow rows, fallen leaf, and spins, including inverted spins, an Immelman, and wingovers. This was why I wanted to be a pilot, but it wasn't a breeze.

The Immelman maneuver follows a high-speed diving attack on an enemy, the attacker climbs back up past the enemy aircraft, and just short of the stall, applies full rudder to twist his aircraft around and put it down at the enemy aircraft, making another high-speed diving pass possible.

It is a difficult maneuver to perform properly, involving precise control of the aircraft at low speed. The wingover is also a difficult maneuver. The air speed at the top and bottom must be consistent with heading changes of one hundred eighty degrees. I did a little sweating up there.

As competent as I was, no one went easy on me. One day, my plane was not at its usual parking spot, which was supposed to be at the north end of the ramp. Going back to the hangar in search of the plane, I found that it had come out of maintenance at the south end of the hangar. Ensign Lewis was waiting in the front cockpit, perturbed that I was late.

The engine required two cranks to start and in the process, boiled over the radiator. Soaking wet and exhausted, I climbed into the rear cockpit, put on my helmet, and plugged in the Gosport hose. Lewis saw me in the mirror and said, "Let's go."

Taxiing to the mat and taking off, he instructed me to climb to altitude for several spins. Then he gave me a high altitude emergency to a power-off landing at one of the outlying fields. I was nervous.

After another takeoff, at four-hundred feet, he simulated an engine failure. I immediately pushed the stick hard forward, as instructed in past training, and found myself hanging onto the stick well out in the slip-stream, unable to move any controls. Lewis saw me in the mirror and pulled the stick back, dumping me back in the seat. My seat belt wasn't fastened. Hurrying to make up time after being late, I had forgotten to buckle up.

When I got back to the barracks, I told Bert I forgot to spit.

Everything was going great for my Stage B check ride. Three goods out of six were required.

I made the first two and the sixth, but the check pilot said I slipped too close to the ground. "That flying is for C stage," the check pilot hollered at me and gave me a down check. I had to fly two additional good rides to pass to the next phase.

Later that day, on my way to ground school, the public address system announced that I had a telegram from the officer of the day. I worried it was bad news of some sort, since it hadn't seemed to be my lucky day, but opening the envelope I read:

In town this weekend—please call,

Mary Elizabeth

I called the general's secretary and made a date for the coming weekend.

She was waiting for me in the lobby of the Adolphus wearing a dark sheath that looked painted on her body. She could have been waiting for the arm of Adolphus Busch himself.

I pulled out the red velvet chair for her in the French Room and sat myself down opposite her. She ordered lamb and because I couldn't read anything on the menu, I said, "I'll have the same." I'd never had lamb before, but it was tasty.

My belly full, I relaxed and reached my arm across the table for Mary Elizabeth's hand. She didn't immediately comply. She looked up at me with raised eyebrows when I asked her if I could read her palm. Before I could show her my talents, her arm swung forward and her hand knocked over my water glass and we both laughed hard. Mary Elizabeth had a loud, raucous laugh that didn't go with her classy appearance, but I liked it. I was hoping it promised at least a good-night kiss.

After paying the bill, I suggested we go to a liquor store and find a place to dance. Texas is a brown bag state—no hard drinks are served—only setups. We found a little place within walking distance of the hotel and I bought the highly advertised Merito Rum and waved down a cab to take us to a club out of the downtown district that had lights strung across the outside dance floor.

Mary pulled me to the dance floor and snuggled up close as we danced to the music of a live band called The Three Bachelors—a piano, bass, and horn. Later, seated at our small table, Mary Elizabeth offered me her hand and said, "I'm not letting you off the hook."

"Oh, I don't want off your hook," I said, taking her hand in mine. She had short fingers that went with the raucous laugh, but not the sleek figure, and I suddenly regretted holding her hand and hoped my disappointment didn't show.

"Tell me what you see," she said winking at me.

"A long life with many children," I said. "But it will only feel long, because of the eight children and five husbands."

"I knew it," she said. "You're a charlatan, an imposter, swindler, and quack!"

"It looks like you're going to be very busy," I said, studying her palm.

"'Looking out for frauds," she answered quickly.

When we got to the bottom of the bottle of rum, we went back to the Aldophus feeling no pain. We took the elevator to Mary's floor. She had stopped calling me Guy and was now calling me Swindler. I don't remember much else.

I woke midmorning entwined with Mary and found my uniform on the floor along with her clothes. I covered a rum stain on a pant leg with the chalk stick I always carried with me and I slipped out the door without leaving a note. I had looked for a piece of paper and a pen to thank her for the evening, but I couldn't find either and gave up. I had a more pressing problem. I had a splitting headache, and for the next two years, I couldn't drink rum.

Gaining confidence in my flying ability, I had more and more time for girls and girls were everywhere, stopping their cars to offer cadets rides to wherever.

"'Where are we going?" I asked, hopping into the car that had pulled over to the curb.

The answer was always, "To a party."

Moving into Stage C training, night flying was added to the program. A battery was installed in the Stearman for cockpit and navigation lights and a flashlight on a cord around the pilot's neck for emergency purposes.

Two parallel lines of five smudge pots were placed on the mat in the direction of the wind to give marginal guidance. Flights were scheduled about sundown, giving some perspective or reference that the pilot might retain in the landing before total darkness.

My first landing was done with an instructor, using a small amount of power to reduce sink rate. After a touch-and-go, I was given control of the plane and the only visual reference to the ground was from the lighted smudge pots. It was wild in a quiet way, because we were surrounded by blackness. The next five were even more fun, because they were solo. It was just me and God in the darkness and I felt God was on my side.

By September 1, 1943, the 22nd had completed their base flying. About ten percent of the starting class washed out but the rest were on their way to Pensacola, Florida, departing Dallas September 25th with seventy-five hours in the Stearman.

I thought I was at the pinnacle of airmanship with little

more to learn piloting an aircraft. How wrong I was. This was only the beginning!

On the way to Pensacola the gun metal gray train made a three-hour stop in New Orleans, giving the men only time to walk several blocks of Canal and Bourbon Street. They arrived in Pensacola late in the afternoon and buses were waiting to take them to Main Side.

NINE

Patrol Bomber
(PBY) - Flying Boat

1943

Pensacola, Florida

T*hrough These Portals Pass the Greatest Aviators in the World* was inscribed on the overhead arch in the Pensacola Theater lobby. Pensacola was a navy town—almost everyone on the sidewalk was in a white uniform.

The 22nd Battalion stay was short. After a physical and a dental check, we received orders to report to Ellyson Field for further flight training. This field was located on the northeast end of Escambia Bay, on the western part of the Florida Panhandle, ringed with campers and young families roasting hotdogs and marshmallows on the ends of sticks held into small beach fires. Here, centuries before, the Spanish explorers brought trinkets to the natives.

It was at Ellyson Field where I was introduced to the SNV airplane, built by Vultee Aircraft in 1941 and used as an intermediate trainer for naval aviators during World War II. The SNV was a more powerful aircraft than the Stearman and a major step in preparing pilots to advance to more complicated, higher performance aircraft. Its annoying harmonics and rattling caused it to be nicknamed the "Vultee Vibrator."

My familiarization flight was with LTJG Myers USNR. All instructors at Pensacola were US Navy or US Navy Reserves and most were designated out of flight training after receiving their wings. Very few had fleet experience or were able to answer questions regarding operations of combat aircraft.

Guy wrote:

Summer gloves and helmets with a built-in headset were added to our flight gear today. We were told the gloves would protect our hands in a bailout—nice to know what lies ahead, though not likely on a familiarization flight.

Lieutenant Myers started the engine and taxied for the takeoff runway, telling me to extend the flaps eleven turns. The prop was in low pitch and with power applied, we started down the runway and lifted off in a gentle left turn. I was impressed by Myers' flying from the rear seat with marginal visibility. He flew the boundaries of the training area and outlying fields that would be used for landing practice and after he demonstrated a landing, it was my turn.

Sitting in the front cockpit with full visibility and a complete instrument panel, I just managed a satisfactory landing. The next two periods were devoted to takeoffs and landings, then a check ride before soloing.

I had four solos before formation instruction with the same procedures that were used in the Stearman. The increased power of the SNV over the Stearman was a thrill. It reminded me of the nervous thrill I got as a kid getting up speed on a swing, so it would fly over the horizontal bar.

Next came formation flights—I had nine of those before my check ride. The pilot assigned to check me was known for having a bad disposition and giving "downs" on days when he got out of bed on the wrong side.

The day before my check with James Cagney, star from *The Public Enemy*, the other instructors put one over on him, making arrangements to have his three students park our planes together as usual, but at a distance from where Cagney was parked at the far end of the ramp, so that the unsuspecting Cagney couldn't see the three instructors take our places in the cockpits after the briefing.

Before Cagney started his engine, the three instructors taxied to the takeoff runway in our planes and took off without an engine run-up and without the use of flaps, staggering into the air, wobbling around in a semi-stall and doing a crossover at low altitude. Cagney was on the radio telling them to return to the field, but they ignored his instructions. They evaded him and returned to the field, landing in a sloppy formation and returning to the line. We cadets then quickly replaced the instructors and waited for the check pilot's arrival. The language Cagney used approaching us was unprintable, but when he discovered the joke was on him, he had the good sense to laugh.

Now, would the prank work to my advantage and motivate James Cagney to prove his reasonableness or the opposite—motivate him to restore his reputation?

I couldn't read him the following day and wasn't sure I'd gotten an up check until I saw it.

On the blackboard the names of Eby, Eichelburger, and

Everett, friends from Dallas, were scheduled to fly together in formation. Nervous, I over-primed my engine causing a large ball of flame to come out of the exhaust by the cockpit, and I bailed out the other side. The fire was of short duration, thank God, and embarrassed for bailing and hoping I hadn't been observed, I jumped back into the cockpit, restarted my engine, and taxied to join Bert and Ike.

All three of us passed the formation check ride and started night flying.

During our training at Ellyson, we selected the type of aircraft we preferred to fly in final squadron, single or multi-engine. Bert, Everett, and I chose multi and were headed for instrument training at Whiting Field in the middle of nowhere, twenty miles from Pensacola.

At Whiting, pilots received instrument training and flew the SNJ airplane, an advanced trainer. Ground school added a new course to the curriculum, RADAR. It was top secret and ID was required before admission was granted to enter the special building containing the gear.

When flying by instruments, it is necessary to discard one's normal instincts for the sensation of turning and the sensation of true vertical. In order to overcome this problem, it is necessary to establish the plane's attitude by the flight instruments and disregard one's senses. After turning three hundred sixty degrees and stopping the turn, Guy had the sensation that he was still turning and was likewise confused into thinking up was down and down was up.

At Whiting, uniform representatives were called to the pilots' quarters. Tailors with their samples of uniforms from different manufacturers located themselves in various rooms with each claiming a better fit, quality, and delivery. Guy ordered a set of tan gabardine and aviation green with two pairs of trousers and blues. Issued blues with the single star on the sleeve were worn as the summer uniform and were the uniform of the day, determined by the area commandant.

At the end of training, the pilots had a choice of flying fighter, torpedo and dive-bomber, or single or multi-engine seaplane. The Catalina PBY multi-engine seaplane was Guy's choice.

December 21st, I had my first flight in the "Flying Boat" with the instructor and flight engineer.

Taxiing in a seaplane is a challenge, as the plane wants to head into the wind. Heading downwind is a balancing act with the throttles, and the more wind the higher degree of difficulty.

Airborne, I headed west to Mobile Bay, a body of water large enough to permit touch-and-go landings and takeoffs without changing heading. I climbed to five hundred feet, and then made a touch-and-go landing.

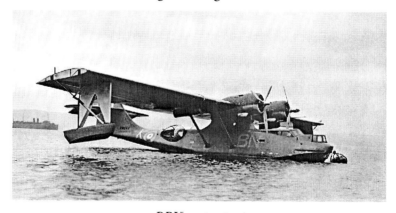

PBY water taxi

I had second thoughts about my decision going into seaplanes, because the PBY with the long wingspan in relation to the fuselage and very large ailerons flew like no other plane. The first several hours flying the PBY, it was impossible to make a coordinated turn.

Disaster struck Christmas Eve. Word reached our quarters that night that an accident had occurred on Perdido Bay. We went down to the seaplane ramp. Lights showed on the water from the crash boat and the *Mary Ann*, the seaplane rescue crane. A small crowd had assembled. The rumor was that two PBYs had crashed with no survivors, each plane carrying four crew members.

The next day it was learned that two separate accidents had occurred. Two planes were practicing night flying in the area. It was a moonless night with only the few lights on shore marking the boundaries of Perdido Bay, plus a string of five buoys with flare pots identifying the touchdown area and wind direction. One PBY entered the landing pattern flying visual and not watching the altitude in the turn, so it dug a wing in the water and water-looped or cartwheeled and burst into flames.

The other flight saw the fire on the water and returned to investigate. Again, flying low in order to view the wreckage, it repeated the accident by digging a float in the water and water-looping. The next several days, wreckage was brought ashore—sections of wings and fuselage.

Christmas was a somber affair having lost so many men in one accident. No one talked. We walked around, because no one could sit still. We played ball, but no one cared about winning and without that desire, there is no point to the game.

Every once in a while, I would catch a look on Everett's face and see what I was feeling—uncertainty—something we rarely felt, mustn't feel, and had to get over feeling.

With twenty hours in the PBY, my roommates and I were scheduled for night flying. After takeoff, the instructor directed me to fly to the beach and then start making turns.

The night was moonless, dark except for lights ashore. There was no problem heading towards the lights ashore. I could see the surf on the beach curl like a ribbon, but as the turn progressed out over the gulf with no visual reference, I experienced vertigo. The plane appeared to me to be stationary and the stars moving. The ultraviolet miniature spotlights shining on the radium instruments produced an eerie glow in the cockpit.

Initially I had trouble keeping the altitude stable, but eventually I was able to stabilize the plane. This particular night experience would turn out to be one of the most important lessons I would learn.

I received my wings and was commissioned Ensign in the Naval Reserve on February 15, 1944. Designated a Naval Aviator, I received orders to the Naval Air Station Banana River.

TEN

Active Duty

1944

Banana River, Florida
Norfolk, Virginia
Harvey Point, North Carolina
Key West, Florida
Alameda, California

We boarded the PBM, Patrol Bomber Martin, on the ramp at Banana River and the signal was given by the ground crewmen to start engines. It was March 27, 1944, and I'd been called to active duty and was onboard with a crew of three students, an instructor, and four crewmen.

The instructor taxied downwind to the takeoff position. The wind was blowing about twenty knots. With the plane heading into the wind, we took off, accelerating with considerably less water noise than the PBY. We skimmed along the water on the step, and at 80 knots, we lifted off the water. Heading north, we banked to the left over the wide Banana River, bringing Merritt Island and the Indian River into view. A few miles north was Cape Canaveral.

The sky and water were big. I felt small in all that blueness, and yet powerful with the mighty force of a multi-engine aircraft under my command. Until that moment, I thought I had made a big mistake electing the multi-engine PBM, but it reaffirmed my choice. The aircraft had better mechanics, greater firepower, and was more comfortable.

Our squadron was permitted off the air station every weekend and a group of us journeyed to Cocoa our first weekend off. The edges of the town were about three blocks in all directions. Like most small Florida towns, Cocoa had only one hotel. It was filled with snowbirds from up north, but the bar was empty. Disappointed, we turned around and took the next bus back to the station.

Only a short distance across the station road was the beach. The main attraction was the pelicans. At an altitude of about one hundred feet, the pelicans' excellent vision enabled them to see fish below the surface. Spotting a fish, they would partially retract their wings, make a minor correction in their dive, extend their bill, retract their wings, and enter the water, striking the fish. They put it in their pouches to feed their young or swallowed it whole. They were superb formation flyers, forming long echelons of forty or more birds.

Formation flying with a PBM was unlike the single-engine planes. I learned to maintain position with millimeter changes with the throttles, a fine-touch training that would prove to be lifesaving.

After six periods of takeoffs and landings, my squadron was able to control the PBM seaplane satisfactorily. My roommate, Springman, and I were often back in our room by four-thirty, playing chess before dinner, but we were at the air station to learn to be fighters.

Our first gunnery flight gave our squadron an opportunity to fire the bow turret guns at a fixed target. They were noisy and created a small amount of acrid-smelling smoke, which drifted into the cockpit.

The bomb bay was filled with hundred-pound water-filled practice bombs. The squadron flew to a fixed target on the water. Approaching the target at one hundred feet and visually estimating the proper time to release the two bombs, I depressed the release button. The crewman at the after hatch observed the explosion of water on water.

While at Banana River, our crew's flight to the naval base at Guantanamo Bay, Cuba, located on the southeastern end of the island, gave us an excellent opportunity to prove navigation theory with a practical application and practice using the radar.

The training continued with more gunnery and bombing—runs were made over the ocean. One of the bombing flights was with live depth charges. The bombs weighed five hundred pounds each and each man had an opportunity to drop and observe the effect on the water. The planes armed with depth charges would be departing on a six-hour triangular course anti-submarine patrol. This was practical training for what we would execute in the war effort—what all our training had been leaning towards.

However, we did manage to have some fun, too—swimming at the beach and playing softball. My days at the Community Center in Hershey, racing Clyde had been a good training ground, but softball was the chosen sport on base and the new men on base included Bob Van.

A batter's first encounter with Bob Van as pitcher was demoralizing. His underhand delivery was as fast as an overhand pitch. Very few batters made contact with the ball.

A game was scheduled, instructors versus students, and naturally Van was picked to pitch for the students. The instructors lost and left the game in a state of shock. A few days later Van's appearance was requested by the commanding officer. It was *suggested* he remain at Banana River as an instructor. On May 15, 1944, my squadron received orders to the Naval Air Station, Norfolk, Virginia, with the exception of Van, who remained behind to pitch softball and instruct.

Days after arriving in Virginia, orders came for us to report to Harvey Point, North Carolina. We boarded a navy bus in the morning after a breakfast of steak and eggs, and arrived late afternoon. Cockpit crews were assigned. Lieutenant Robert S. Scott was the number three man by seniority—he had gone through flight training after having his ship sunk during the battle of the Coral Sea. His flying experience was less than the other plane commanders, but his knowledge of navy regulations and procedures exceeded the officers junior to him. Dompier and I were assigned to his crew—we alternated positions during patrols copiloting one flight and navigating the next.

Except for those on night flying or with the duty, the workday ended at 1600 hours. Those who lived off-base would hurry home to their brides. The rest of us would find fellowship at the officers' club over a few beers.

By August, the twelve aircraft were headed for Key West for two weeks of intensive training in anti-submarine warfare by the Boca Chica training unit. The sona-buoy was introduced, a cylinder three feet long with a transmitter attached to a microphone on a long cable, permitting the aircraft to listen in on submarine sounds emanating from the water.

Guy wrote:

We listened to sinister low bell tones and sonar pings that were eerie and put us in a dark underwater world of echoes, a chilling world. Better to be in the sky than under the sea.

The PBM was capable of carrying two torpedoes. The copilot instructed the pilot to turn left or right while looking through the sight, keeping the cross hair on the target. Torpedoes were dropped at two thousand yards from the target at an altitude of two hundred feet.

Additional bombing runs were made on towed targets, improving our proficiency until the big day arrived when we dropped live, unarmed torpedoes on a towed target.

Three miles from the target, we began a descent and aligned the crosshairs. At two thousand yards and two hundred feet, the torpedo was released, nosing over and contacting the water the instant the alcohol boiler was activated.

The steam turbine propelled the torpedo toward the target, running hot and true as observed from the air in the clear water. Without a warhead, the torpedo floated to the surface and was retrieved.

The return flight to Harvey Point on 23 August was uneventful. A seaplane tender was positioned in the eastern bay of the Chesapeake for a rendezvous with our squadron to familiarize operating with a tender. Our crew had an opportunity to take on fuel from the stern of the AVP Auxiliary Seaplane

Tender and practiced securing the plane to a mooring.

By late September, my squadron was ready to shove off for the West Coast. In five plane sections, our squadron began departing for Naval Air Station Alameda the morning of 28 September.

Alameda was, in effect, a jumping off point, which could be said about all the bases where I trained. The goal was Hawaii, a Trans-Pacific Flight.

We boarded the plane and put over the side into the water at 2130. Lieutenant Scott taxied to the takeoff area, checked the engines, and waited for the other PBMs in the flight to be ready for departure.

Takeoff power was applied and slowly we increased air speed. We were under the Bay Bridge before we were airborne. Climbing through a thin layer of fog with the lights of San Francisco on the left, we could see the Top of the Mark above the fog.

One night weeks before, I had been sitting across the table from a beautiful woman in the Mark. When I saw the tip of the grand hotel above the fog, I pictured Shirley's auburn hair and thought I could smell the soap she had used. It was a fleeting sensation interrupted by the slow climbing out of the harbor toward the Golden Gate, where we passed between the two bridge towers like a pigskin sailing over the goal posts.

Over the Pacific Ocean, we climbed to eight thousand feet, our cruising altitude. Twenty minutes later, we made radio contact with the other planes that were airborne. The outside air temperature was forty degrees, so inside the plane, the crew members were cold with only medium-weight flight jackets to keep warm. Unnoticed on previous flights, now cold air blew through the flight deck, entering under the instrument panel and around the rudder pedals. Air leaks around the bow turret forced the cold air through the fuselage like a small wind tunnel. Closing the entrance door and opening the galley allowed the air to pass through the galley, thus, reducing the cold air moving through the flight deck.

Dompier and I alternated positions between copilot and navigator; I navigated the first flight to Kaneoha. Navigating occupied time better than sitting in the cockpit watching the gauges and trying to keep warm. The sky was overcast during the first two hours into the flight, so only dead reckoning assumed our position on the chart. Finally the stars were visible, so it was possible to take a celestial sight.

Forward of the deck turret, a second deck over the bunks was the location of the auxiliary power unit (APU) and the exit hatch between the wings. Within the hatch cover was an

PBM cockpit

astrodome, which allowed three-hundred-sixty-degree coverage for celestial sights. I climbed up onto the APU deck and placed the octant in the support fixture of the dome. I took a three-star fix, selecting three stars approximately one hundred and twenty degrees apart. This plots three lines of position which form a triangle—the smaller the triangle, the more accurate the fix. It took fifteen minutes to leave the navigation table, go to the astrodome, take three sights, and return and plot. The fix placed us fifteen miles south and five miles behind the dead reckoning position. A minor heading change was made to the north and a new estimate given for the next required radio position report.

Scotty took a celestial fix to confirm my navigation, putting his fix within a few miles of my estimated position. The sun was rising behind us, a yellow and rose strip of color at the horizon, stars no longer visible. My last star fix was a half-hour earlier. The plane began to be warmed by the rising sun and one of the crewmen started cooking breakfast—steak and eggs with fresh coffee. The galley seated two lucky son of a guns who were warmed by the additional heat of the electric stove.

Flying above the overcast, the radar confirmed our position as fifty miles from destination. We descended through the overcast, and leveled off at one thousand feet with the shoreline in view. Entering the landing pattern the mountain, several miles beyond the seaplane area, was a vertical corrugated wall three thousand feet above sea level. Turning left to the north, Scotty lined up on the windows on the water and we touched down fifteen hours and forty minutes after takeoff from San Francisco Bay. The return trip to Oakland was uneventful—it took eleven hours.

At the 7 November muster, after only a few hours of sleep, the crew was scheduled for a test flight to Kaneohe that night. Dampier was the navigator this time and I was the copilot. The flight back to Oakland and the bus ride to Alameda were uneventful. On the next flight to Kaneohe, our final, we would not be returning to the Bay area. At muster on December 8, 1944, we were informed that conditions were favorable, so we would be flying to Kaneohe, Hawaii, that evening.

ELEVEN

Near Disaster

1945

Pacific Theatre

On July 3, 1945, Lieutenant (jg) Kohler's crew and mine were assigned to patrol a sector twenty miles east of the China mainland in the East China Sea, then into the Yellow Sea to the area near Ch'ingtao and return. It was my turn to navigate and Scott's turn to take off, while Dompier occupied the copilot's seat. Three-foot swells were moving through the takeoff area and the seaplane made two bounces before becoming airborne. The lieutenant and his crew took off and joined up in a loose formation on their northwest heading.

Cruising at two thousand feet after two-and-a-half hours, they were twenty miles east of Pako Lieh-tao (Parker Islands), the eastern boundary of Hangchou Wan (Bay). Radio silence between the two planes had been maintained. Only negative contact and their position messages had been forwarded to the fleet. Scott decided to search the area of the bay, so he changed course to the west.

Approaching the mouth of the Yangtze River with its yellow

water, a tug towing a barge low in the water was sighted entering the bay. Scott ordered the ordinance man to set two one-hundred-pounders on the intervalometer. Without informing Kohler of his intentions, Scott started to descend. Heading for the tug, he ordered the fifty-caliber guns to fire when in range. Crossing over the tug, the two bombs were dropped short. Following behind, one of Kohler's one-hundred-pounders scored a hit leaving the tug dead in the water. Scott circled for a second pass, lining up on the tug, but again dropped short. Leaving the sinking tug, Scott took a heading southwest, paralleling the dark mainland shore, and climbed to one thousand feet.

The fifty-caliber guns on the PBM could jam after one or two bursts of fire. The rounds were fed from a receptacle feed rack that led to the guns. Being in the hostile environment of salt air, the steel links that belted the brass cartridges together corroded and would not permit the links to slide free before entering the chamber of the gun, causing it to jam.

At the flight engineer's panel, Miller asked me to relieve him, so he could go aft and help clear the guns. Kohler had again joined up in loose formation, when suddenly our pilot, Scott, saw enemy aircraft coming down out of the sun. The lead plane, a dark streak like an arrow, had shot out of the golden ball of light, an engaging effect, but lethal.

Kohler was watching the black explosions above and ahead. Then both pilots saw small parachutes floating down from the black explosions, and hanging from the parachutes were wires that held explosives. About twelve anti-aircraft shells, which looked to be 40mm fire, cut through the PBMs intended flight path. Over the intercom, Dompier alerted everyone, "Fighters 12 o'clock high."

Scott dove for the water. The bow turret opened fire, and moments later, with a sound like a large paper bag exploding, white smoke filled the cockpit and was quickly exhausted through the flight deck.

Something had hit just aft of the bow turret and exploded. The plane was diving toward the water. Scott was struggling at the controls, as I moved toward the cockpit and saw that most of the flight instruments in the left panel were missing. Scott appeared to have been hit by a shotgun loaded with watch parts and was in a state of shock. His left knee had an exposed hole in the bone the size of a half dollar.

I was unaware that Dompier, our copilot, had been hit above the left eye and was blinded by the hemorrhaging blood, because he still knew to pull back on the control column. However, the seaplane was diving for the water.

I tapped him on the shoulder, signaling I was there to relieve him. Dompier extracted himself from the seat and I took his place and immediately pulled back on the control column, which came back effortlessly, but the plane continued its dive.

Reaching over to the elevator trim tab, located inboard of the left seat, I gave it a spin-up. The PBM responded abruptly, going from a dive to a climb less than a hundred feet above the yellow water.

Leveling off at three hundred feet, I started a turn to take us out to sea, but discovered the up elevator and rudder controls were inoperative. Dompier, in his hasty retreat, took along his headset. The radioman handed a headset forward to me and I heard Kohler say, "Scott, come back and help us. All the fighters are making runs on us."

I explained I had limited control and was heading out to sea. Miller returned to the flight deck and removed Scott to the bunk room for first aid. The other injured crew members were Monroe, an ordinance man who had been standing between the pilots' seats when he received a superficial wound on the face, and Epperly, the tail gunner, who lost a piece of heel bone from shrapnel.

Five Tojo fighters from the China mainland had intersected our flight. The Tojo's armament was a 9 mm machine gun firing through the propeller, to line up the ten 40 mm, which fired through the propeller shaft.

My plane took five 40 mm shells. The one that entered just above the bow turret exploded back of the left instrument panel. The second entered the right wing between the fuselage and the engine, exploding ahead of the self-sealing fuel cell. The third entered the fuselage ahead of the tail turret and exploded by the bell crank for the elevator, severing the elevator and rudder cables, and injuring the tail gunner. Two additional shells did superficial damage to the horizontal stabilizer and elevator. The trim tab system on the PBM was a torque shaft, which was perforated by the explosion.

Out at sea, Kohler joined up. I reported their condition and requested that I lead the flight back to Kerama Retto. Kohler had an excessively rich running engine with black smoke coming out of the exhaust. The Tojo fighters thought he was a wounded duck and devoted all their attention to his plane, which saved my plane from further attack.

Miller came forward to tell me that Scott was losing a lot of blood and needed something to block the artery above his knee. I gave him one of my cigars, which was placed in the tourniquet, reducing the flow.

Voice communication between Kohler and me was intercepted by a friendly submarine on their course. The sub offered medical assistance, if we landed at sea. That was impractical, as there were just two more hours to base and a marginally controllable aircraft attempting an open sea landing would have been too risky. Air Wing was advised that Scott would need plasma after landing and I requested medical assistance be standing by for our landing.

Approaching the landing area, Sea Drome Control cleared me to land by the re-arming boat in the landing area. I remained in the right seat, somewhat unfamiliar, because takeoff and landings were always flown from the left seat. However, the left instrument panel's flight instruments had been removed by the 40 mm explosion, which required us to use the copilot's panel. Miller spliced the up elevator cable, but was unable to exert the necessary tension, resulting in about a three-inch free movement of the control column.

Our approach had to be made using excessive up trim and holding forward pressure on the control column. I had intended to make a power-on partial stall landing, but entering the ground cushion, the nose dropped, releasing the back pressure, and so I failed to bring the nose up sufficiently. The PBM hit the water making a low bounce. Pulling back on the column, Miller's splice held and we settled back into the water. The engines were stopped and a flat-bottomed re-arming boat with corpsman and a doctor came alongside.

Scott was given plasma before being removed from the plane and received more plasma on the stretcher—seven pints total. Scott, Dompier, and Epperly were taken directly to the hospital ship. I tried to taxi to the mooring buoy, but was unable to start the right engine and had to be towed. During the repair to the battle-damaged sea plane, the mechanics found that the shell that entered the leading edge of the right wing had severed the mixture control cable.

On board the tender, the ship's doctor requested I come to sickbay. There he opened a locked cabinet, which contained liquor for medicinal purposes and said, "I think you need a drink."

"I don't need one," I answered, "but I will take one!"

The next day, I went to visit the injured crew members on the hospital ship. In addition to his critical knee injury, Scott had a dangerous shrapnel wound in his left chest, restricting the flow of blood through an artery. With all his discomfort, he still was in good spirits, joking about his visibly pulsating artery and the audible sound of blood passing by the restriction. He also had superficial wounds on his fingers, face, and chest caused by fragments of the instruments and panel. I would have spent more time with Scott, but the strong odor of antiseptic in the ward made me light-headed and I had to leave.

Dompier had a cut above the eye and an internal eye injury. Epperly was airlifted to the Naval Hospital on Guam for treatment. Dompier returned to the Yakutat the following day with an eye patch. Days later, he complained of partial vision in the injured eye.

On 18 July, Dompier had orders to the Naval Hospital at Pearl Harbor. Later he was admitted to a naval hospital stateside and received a medical discharge. Scott was airlifted back to the states after a short time in Guam and Pearl for a bone grafting and extended stay in Los Angeles. Finally he was sent to the San Francisco area and discharged over a year after his injuries as an outpatient.

Captain Chase summoned me to his cabin and proposed that I continue with Scott's crew as the plane commander.

Captain Eby

TWELVE

American Airlines

November 1975 (30 Years Later)

Connecticut

The bid sheet from American Airlines was laying on the yellow Formica countertop in a return white envelope. My wife, Barbara, passed through the kitchen on her way to the back door and gathered it up with the other mail to go out that morning. She called to me in the laundry room that she wouldn't be long, but I heard only a rumble of words. After replacing the last screw in the back panel of the washer, I turned on the water.

Talking to our grown boys on the phone the night before, Barbara and I decided to spend Thanksgiving at home in Connecticut, which freed me up to fly out of Kennedy on the 25th to San Francisco and after a short layover fly to Chicago, pick up passengers and continue on to Newark where I would get a limousine to Kennedy and drive home to Connecticut late that night. If I was lucky and there wasn't too much traffic, I would fall asleep before the sun rose on Thanksgiving Day.

The round trip out of Kennedy to San Francisco was a good

flight. Not only did it pay well, it was a long flight. After 25 years flying for American, I was having as much fun as I did on my first commercial flight in 1950 when I left the navy. It was always a thrill to sit in the cockpit, face that wide expanse of the night sky, and dive into the mystery beyond. It was a different experience in the daytime, climbing above the clouds to an azure blue sky and bright sunlight was wonderful in its own way, but not as thrilling, not mysterious. The darkness gave me the feeling of endlessness and maybe even immortality.

THIRTEEN

The Passenger

November 1975

Oak Brook, Illinois

Business and personal commitments prevented my family and me from leaving Chicago for Thanksgiving in Connecticut earlier on the 26th. Three airlines had flights out of Chicago to New York that day, but only two of those had the five seats we needed and only one had the five consecutive seats—American Airlines. I booked us on flight 182, scheduled to leave O'Hare at 4:40 p.m. on the 26th of November to arrive at Newark Airport around 7:38 p.m.

Our plan was to get a cab at Newark Airport and stay overnight at my sister Judy's place on 12th Street in Greenwich Village. Thanksgiving morning, we would drive with Judy to my brother Ted's house in Greenwich, Connecticut. The weather forecast was for cold and possibly snowy weather, which was my main concern. We had no way of knowing the drama that awaited us.

FOURTEEN

First Leg

7:00 a.m. November 26, 1975

Kennedy Airport

I stood in the Ready Room looking over weather forecasts and recent accident and near accident reports as I waited for the copilot and engineer to arrive. I was early, but then, I was always early. I had been flying for American Airlines for twenty-five years and I would guess that in those years, I'd read more than a thousand accident reports, but I was still a cheerful

man. There was nothing maudlin about me—I was fascinated by those reports. I was always curious about the challenges, human, mechanical, and weather that caused a plane to veer off a runway, lose an engine in flight, or overcome power loss due to flocks of birds being sucked into an engine.

Ready room

FIFTEEN

First Hours

7:00 a.m. November 26, 1975

Oak Brook, Illinois

Iknew before I got out of bed that it was a cold morning. I heard the furnace turn on in the middle of the night and was unable to fall back to sleep. I had a lot to do before we left for the Thanksgiving weekend and the week that followed, visiting family and friends in Boston. I slipped my arms into the sleeves of my robe and went to my desk to gather up files to take with me, maybe read on the plane.

Several hours later at my office, writing notes to myself that I tucked into my briefcase, my wife, Elaine, called to ask if I had arranged the taxi, what time would it pick us up, and did the taxi know there were five of us with luggage, so we would need a large taxi?

When she hung up the phone, Elaine returned to the kitchen table where our three kids were eating their favorite breakfast, French toast made with homemade challah, bacon, and hot chocolate. I could imagine them talking fast and inter-rupting one another, excited about seeing their cousins the next day. They had missed most family Thanksgivings, because our extended family lived back east in New York, Connecticut, and Boston.

I imagined Elaine, busy organizing the family and getting caught up in the kids' enthusiam for and anticipation of the week ahead. They were especially eager to sleep over in Aunt Judy's fourth floor walk-up.

SIXTEEN

One Down

10:00 a.m.

San Francisco, California

The jumbo jet from Kennedy flew in over the Bay and touched down on the runway in fog that the sun hadn't entirely burned off.

SEVENTEEN

Starting Out

1:00 p.m.

Oak Brook, Illinois

Laurence cleared the table of the paper plates used for lunch and threw them into the waste basket, then took the plastic bag to the garage. When he returned to the kitchen, he asked, "What happened to all the trash from yesterday? The garbage can is empty."

"We're going away," his sister, Laura, reminded him.

He knew that. They just ate lunch on paper plates to save time for last minute things like opening the faucets to dribble water and prevent the pipes from freezing. But why no trash in the garage?

"Rather than leave the refuse in the garage all week, your dad took it to the office dumpster this morning," his mother said.

The morning was spent packing and moving from room to room, picking up this and closing up that, while I wrapped up things at the office. And when I got home: "Don't forget your homework for the plane ride," and "The cab will be here soon. You need to get a move on. Everyone, please organize and set by the front door the items you're taking, so that we can make sure we've got it all."

The four of them in the back seat were shoulder to shoulder sandwiched into the taxi with their jackets on their laps, while I sat up front with the driver. The children were in high spirits next to Elaine, who was quiet—no doubt worried that she had forgotten to pack something or remind me to stop the news-paper. Leslie, beside her, removed her jacket from her lap and tucked it down behind her legs. "It must be a hundred degrees in here," she said softly, knowing it would be inconsiderate if the taxi driver heard her complaint.

"It's only a half an hour to the airport," Elaine reassured her. "Think about something else," she said.

At the American Airlines terminal, we toppled out of the cab and shook off the heat as we took in a breath of fresh air.

"It's snowing," Laurence realized.

Laura had her eyes closed and her chin up, looking like she was enjoying the sensation of the snowflakes landing gently on her cheeks.

"Do you suppose it is snowing in New York and Connecticut?" Leslie asked no one in particular.

"The farmer's almanac says we are due for a cold and snowy winter," the taxi driver said as he took the bills from me and wished us a safe trip and a Happy Thanksgiving.

EIGHTEEN

Flight 182

1975

2:00 p.m. O'Hare Airport, Chicago, Illinois

I got off the plane in Chicago and did a visual check of it from the ground, stepping around the wheels, inspecting the landing gear, and standing under the jets, looking up into the turbines for streaks of oil, loose or missing bolts, or any signs of potential problems. I was well aware of the DC-10's poor safety record, especially in its earlier operations, and the design flaw in the cargo doors. Two weeks before flight 182, on November 12, 1975, a DC-10 had struck a flock of seagulls while taking off from New York's JFK and while the captain aborted, the #3 engine exploded causing partial braking failure. The landing gear collapsed and fire destroyed the aircraft. Fortunately all 139 aboard survived. I was aware of what could go wrong and was incredibly vigilant long before I took over the controls.

Minutes later in the terminal, I called Barbara and apologized for not calling from San Francisco. I'd lost track of time talking to a mechanic about a new attitude indicator he had ordered for my Swift. When I wasn't flying the jumbo jets for

Guy and Swift

American, I was flying my Swift or thinking about it.

Barbara sounded anxious on the phone. Not about my day. She knew I was safest up in the airspace. She was anxious about the next day's big meal. I was distracted—something about the attitude indicator I didn't understand and the mechanic in San Francisco couldn't explain. I was like a dog with a bone when I wanted an answer to a mechanical or electrical problem.

Flying had always come naturally to me, but that feeling didn't make me overly confident. I'd spent my life learning everything there was to learn about airplanes and the skies I flew in, but that doesn't mean I wasn't instinctual about it. I could fly for hours without a worry, barely having to think what I was doing and, paradoxically, I was always thinking what to do next if this or that happened. I felt carefree flying unless I was flying for someone. Then it was a job and I was thinking about my responsibility to my passengers. They expect me to be thinking about what I was doing every minute of the flight. Readiness was my rule.

NINETEEN

Boarding

4:40 p.m.

O'Hare Airport

It was announced that our flight was delayed due to mechanical problems.

In deference to my bad habit, our Herman family was seated in row 28 of the smoking section at the back of the plane, with fourteen-year-old Laurence and forty-four year-old me in seats A and B, while Elaine and the twelve-year-old girls, Leslie and Laura, were in seats C, D, and E. The plane was packed without room to spare in the overhead compartments or under the seats. Laurence slid a school book under the seat in front of him. I tucked my briefcase in under the seat beside that. Leslie used her foot to push her backpack under the seat in front of her and Laura complained the backpack was taking up space where her feet belonged. I saw Elaine reach over and pull the pink backpack out and push it under the seat in front of her to settle things before they got started.

The seat belt sign was turned on. I looked to see if my son's was fastened as the senior flight attendant, Sandra completed her pre-flight spiel with, "On behalf of Captain Eby and our entire New York-based flight crew, welcome aboard American Airlines continuing flight 182, non-stop to Newark International."

Out my window the runway lights flashed and sparkled in the dark, some intermittently and some steadily. It was festive-looking. The runway had a dusting of snow, looking like it had received a fine spray of white paint.

American Airlines Flight 182 lifted off, cut into, and was swallowed up by thick clouds that reflected back the light from the airplane's nose gear and wings. At this hour on a clear November night in Chicago, the sky would have been pitch-black dotted with stars.

My family didn't know that our plane would be one of the last to leave O'Hare that night, but we would later learn that our pilot, Guy Eby, knew from the look and feel of the runway, the storm clouds out his windscreen, and the forecast for heavy snow over the Midwest and East, that he was likely to be one of the last pilots flying out of O'Hare that night, and was feeling lucky to have slipped through that hole in the fence.

TWENTY

Near Collision

7:15 p.m.

In the cockpit above Lake Michigan

The thickening clouds above southwest Michigan were becoming a nuisance, "like driving down a country road in a heavy fog." I thought I might escape them by flying higher, so I asked permission to lift above 28,000 feet. I was given permission to ascend to 33,000 feet and maintain. Then I was cleared to 37,000 feet.

At the same time I was making my ascent, I could hear a TWA pilot over the radio describe the same cloud cover my plane was in. Thinking out loud I said, "I wonder where he is?"

At 7:22 p.m., the control center at Cleveland was going through a shift change, so the new controller needed a few moments to fully absorb what he was seeing on his screen: two jumbo jets, an American DC10 and a TWA L1011, American Flight 182 heading east and TWA Flight 37 cruising west. American's altitude was slightly lower, but its upward trajectory was moving it directly into the path of the TWA L1011.

However, I didn't know what controller Hewitt knew— that two jumbo jets, traveling at a combined speed of nearly 1000 mph, were headed on a course that would intersect. Hewitt didn't believe his eyes and radioed my DC 10.

"American 182, Cleveland, say your altitude."

I responded, "Passing through three four point seven at this time. We're still in the area of clouds, but can see stars above."

Hewitt issued this urgent command, "American 182, descend immediately to 330!"

At that moment, I saw a glow of light beyond my plane's windscreen—the lights of the L1011.

"There he is," I said to my copilot as I pushed the yoke violently forward, deactivating the auto pilot. Then pushed the yoke hard a second time to make a sudden 35 degree descent and drop more than a thousand feet with a negative g-force lasting six seconds.

The mock speed warning, sounding like a hundred loud chickens clucking, was triggered.

Back in the cabin we were drinking cokes, sipping coffee, and nibbling on airline snacks. As soon as the No Smoking light was turned off, I lit up a Lark cigarette as the flight attendants were starting the dinner service of lasagna. And then all hell broke loose. Passengers, crew members, cocktail carts, dinner trays, and glasses were hurled into the chaos of weightlessness. My son Laurence shot out of his seat. I instinctively lunged for him, but couldn't hold him down. His head hit the overhead compartment. I was unaware that he had unfastened his seat belt. Elaine and I shared a fateful look that we were about to die. With eyes wide open and in silent scream I felt so helpless, at the mercy of forces beyond my control. There was screaming and moaning from those who still had their voices.

Oxygen masks fell, although the plane never lost pressurization. Later the crew referred to this as the "rubber jungle." Hot and cold liquids splashed and lasagna dinners splattered. Stewardesses were flung to the ceiling and one of them crashed through to the underside of the fuselage.

And if that wasn't enough to scare the beejebers out of me, some of the overhead panels that were knocked loose were tethered by wires revealing the innards of our aircraft and raising doubt about the worthiness of our airplane.

John Ruffley, 51, an engineer from Summit, New Jersey, who suffered a badly bruised arm said, "We were eating dinner, when we were suddenly hurled from our seats. Food was tossed around the cabin. It was a mess. People were thrown to the ceiling and fell back down on other passengers. Panels were torn from the ceiling and sewage from the toilets flowed down the aisles. Hinges were broken off escape doors. It was lucky we didn't depressurize."

Mrs. William Brady of LaGrange, Illinois who escaped injury, told a newspaper reporter, "One minute everything is fine and the next it's chaos."

Another passenger said, "It was like riding the tail end of a snapping whip."

A Chicago public aid caseworker and Loyola University night school law student on her way to visit her parents in New Jersey said, "The plane began to fall. We were just sitting there and without notice, I started to slide out of my seat. Then I hit the ceiling and hit the floor." The 24-year-old who would one day be an Illinois judge, sustained a huge gash in her knee. She was one of the 26 injured, taken to Wayne County General Hospital.

Marla Schor, a 20-year-old Northwestern University student from New Jersey, who was seated near us at the rear of the aircraft said, "I had unfastened my seat belt soon after takeoff and quickly dozed off. At first I imagined I was dreaming, as I flew about the cabin in a state of weightlessness." Badly injured, Marla was removed by stretcher.

Passengers who were seated at the rear of the aircraft as we were experienced the worst of the plunge. From my vantage point, I witnessed the kind of pandemonium you see in a movie. But this was real life.

It was like a roller coaster ride with its parabolic hills. What a petrifying feeling, dropping more than a thousand feet, in a nose-down jumbo jet in a matter of seconds and the paralyzing, heart-pounding, gut-wrenching conviction that we were all about to die. And there was nothing—absolutely nothing—I could do about it but pray. I whispered, "*Please, God.*" And in those brief otherworldly moments, I couldn't help but wonder, "*Is this how it all ends? If we're going to die, let it be quick and painless.*" I couldn't bear to see my family suffer, unable to hold them tight and tell them how much I loved them and calm their fright.

In the cockpit I had to lift the plane out of the dive before the wings tore off the fuselage and the engines stalled, and before a condition called "red out" overcame us, which is a pooling of blood in the eyes and head, with loss of consciousness. I had done this lift before off the Yangtze Cape in '45. I pulled the yoke back and about 500,000 pounds of steel pulled up, restoring gravity. However, everything that had been weightless, floating in the cabin, suddenly came crashing down to the floor and seats, where terrified passengers sat vulnerable. Some passengers and flight attendants were severely injured, suffering head injuries, back injuries, broken bones, and lacerations from flying objects that had pierced their flesh.

The moment I stabilized the DC 10, I shut off the flight recorder to save what had been recorded. Left to keep recording, it would have recorded over those minutes of horror, because the flight recorder only had a half-hour of recording time before it recycled.

The next thing I did was call for an emergency landing in Detroit so that the injured could be taken to the hospital for treatment. I didn't tell the dispatcher what had happened, because that would have sent every reporter in Detroit to the airport. And I didn't tell the passengers the reason for our sudden dive.

When I stepped out of the cockpit and scanned the chaos of the cabin, I saw red splotches on the ceiling, on the walls, the seats—red stains were everywhere. It was very emotional. I knew there were injured passengers, and some had to be removed by stretcher. However I wouldn't know until the next day that some splatters of red were also from the lasagna that was served at the time of our plunge.

I called my family and spoke longest to my oldest son, Robert, who was also a pilot. We have had many conversations about the 200-pound service carts that could become flying wreckers doing the most harm to cabin and passengers.

Something else troubled me. I questioned myself: *Should I have told the passengers what caused me to send the plane into a dive?*

We heard only this terse, but reassuring voice over the intercom, "This is Captain Eby speaking. Our aircraft is structurally sound and we've been cleared for an emergency landing at Detroit's Metropolitan Airport."

Despite Captain Eby's assurances and given the disorder of our cabin, it didn't seem possible that the plane was capable of a safe landing. But several minutes later, the most beautiful sight I have ever seen, landing lights and the flashing red and blue lights of emergency vehicles, came into view as we landed to a chorus of cheers and applause of the grateful passengers.

Twenty-six passengers and crew were removed by paramedics, some by stretcher, and taken to area hospitals. The rest of us remained seated until the debris was cleared from the aisles. Then we were escorted from the shambles of the cabin, tiptoeing over the toilet detritus to a private area of the terminal where, for the longest time, we were told nothing. We milled around speculating about one thing and another: Was it wind shear? An air pocket? Turbulence? Aircraft malfunction? Stricken pilots?

Waiting on word, I thought about this proposition: when the aircraft door closed, my life was now in the hands of people I didn't know—people I would probably never see again. I was just a bystander along for the ride. I would later learn that when I purchased my ticket, I entered into what is known as a *contract of carriage*, addressing a multitude of topics such as liability and acts of God. I never read that lengthy document. In fact, I never knew it existed. I'm sure I'm not the only one.

Guy Eby is a Scorpio (November 9th). You may know that Scorpios are said to be focused, brave, balanced, intuitive, and are all about control. For a Scorpio to be out of control is very disturbing, even dangerous. I know! I'm a Scorpio. And I'm eternally grateful a Scorpio was at the controls of our DC-10, a name that was once mocked as an abbreviation for *death cruiser* or *Douglas coffin* for its many fatal accidents during its thirty-year commercial flying history.

After more than an hour, American offered us pas-
sangers three options, as O'Hare was shut down because of
a snowstorm:

- Bus us back to Chicago
- Fly on to Newark on another plane that night as
  soon as one became available
- Stay overnight in a Detroit hotel and fly to Newark
  in the morning

We elected to fly to Newark as soon as a plane was available. Passengers that were released from the hospital, but
wanted to do the same had returned to the airport.

I believe in the adage, if you fall off a horse, you need to
get right back on. I was concerned if we didn't, my children
might develop a fear of flying. That is, if they hadn't already.
Besides, at the time, we were clueless about the cause of our
violent descent. If we knew, it's likely we might have decided
differently.

Unknown by us at the time, the Vice President of Flight
Operations asked the co-pilot, "Do you think Guy can continue?" His answer was, "He seems normal to me." Then
Guy was asked the same question. He smiled and said, "Of
course I can." A few hours later, we were on another plane,
piloted by Guy Eby.

A few days later, Guy received this note:

AmericanAirlines

In Flight...

Altitude;

Location;

Dear Capt. Eby,

Just wanted to let you know all the girls seem to be doing fine — some of us are a little stiff and will be out of work a while — but that's not all bad. I just wanted to say on behalf of myself, my family and my friends — thank you for taking the action you did Wed. night — you made this a true Thanksgiving. I'm so glad to be here

Sandra Olsauer
Flt Attndt #5
Flight #182
LGA

More than four decades later that close encounter is still referred to as an air disaster that didn't happen.

B6 Sunday, February 12, 2017 | Herald-Tribune *S* | heraldtribune.com

THE 1975 AIR DISASTER THAT WASN'T

Only one member of the TWA cockpit crew, the flight engineer, had seen the lights of the descending American, which appeared close enough to reach out and touch. TWA flight 37 from Philadelphia continued uneventfully to Los Angeles. When the flight engineer told his pilot he had seen the tail-lights of a DC 10, he was told that was impossible—that he had imagined it. It wasn't possible that there could be another plane in their airspace.

The passengers of American Airlines 182 wouldn't know about TWA Flight 37 until the following day

What could have been the worst mid-air aircraft against aircraft disaster in US aviation history, a death toll exceeding 300 people one day before Thanksgiving, had been averted by a cool, highly trained pilot who knew what to do and did it masterfully. What many never came to realize, because the media did not point it out—the dive at the moment before impact, was only the first remarkable action. The second was Captain Eby's ability to safely pull us out of the dive.

TWENTY-ONE

Thanksgiving Morning

1975

I-95 North to Greenwich, Connecticut and LaGuardia Airport

Driving to Greenwich, we turned on the car radio and for the first time heard the spine-tingling details of a near air collision of two jumbo jets over Carleton, Michigan.

"Last night in the skies over Michigan, TWA flight 37, heading west from Philadelphia to Los Angeles, and American Airlines Flight 182, heading east from Chicago to Newark, came within 20 feet of each other in what could have been the worst midair collision of two jumbo airplanes in the history of commercial aviation."

A staccato of voices cried out, "Oh, my God! My God! Oh, my God!"

On the Captain's Irregularity Report, Captain Eby stated, "I was the Captain of AA Flight 182 on November 26, 1975. While on Cleveland Air Traffic Control frequency, we were cleared to FL 330. Before reaching FL330, we were re-cleared to climb to FL370. Approaching or going through FL350, we were instructed to "descend immediately to FL330." Instantly I started a descent with the autopilot vertical speed control. Simultaneously I sighted another aircraft at 12 o'clock in the opposite direction. I manually increased nose down and then further increased forward pressure to avoid the other aircraft. From sighting to passing of the other aircraft overhead, estimate time 3 to 4 seconds. Estimate distance between aircraft at passing, less than 100 feet vertically."

Captain Eby provided technical data and ended his report explaining that when he leveled off, he informed the passengers that the airplane was structurally sound and an emergency landing would be made at Detroit's Metropolitan Airport.

The NTSB concluded that the probable cause of the near-collision was the controller's failure to use prescribed separation criteria when he first became aware of the conflict, maintaining that Drew Parker, the Cleveland radar controller, failed to order course changes to separate the planes, thinking that one of the planes might level off or change course slightly on its own, as several other craft on similar flight paths had done that day.

The report stated that Parker then became distracted and forgot about the two jets. Minutes before the two planes on track to collide reached that point in the night sky, Parker was relieved by Charles Hewitt, who had been on break. In briefing Hewitt, Parker failed to mention TWA 37 and AA 182.

When controller Hewitt took over and saw on his radar screen the two planes closing in on each other, he said he didn't believe his eyes. But instead of ordering AA 182 to descend immediately, he radioed Captain Eby asking his altitude, and by the time Hewitt ordered AA 182 to immediately descend, Guy was already looking at the lights of TWA 37 across his windscreen and had plunged the yoke forward.

Perhaps Hewitt was a believer in Cosmic Awareness that teaches one "not to believe anything, but to question, explore, doubt, and discover for yourself what the truth is." All well and good, except if you are an air traffic controller, you had better believe what you're seeing, and quickly.

Given that air traffic controllers are exquisitely trained to maintain the safe, orderly, and expeditious flow of air traffic in their sector, Parker's and Hewitt's diminished situational awareness was enigmatic.

Accounts were reported in the local and national media, including *Time Magazine*, the *New York Times*, the *Baltimore Sun*, and the *Washington Star*.

So how close did we come in real time?

According to my grandson, a math whiz, two planes racing toward each other at a combined speed of nearly 1,000 miles per hour and missing by 20 feet is a fraction of a second. The blink of an eye.

Thanks to Captain Eby, a cataclysmic event was narrowly averted over the small farming community of Carleton, Michigan. Carleton took its name from its favorite son, Will Carleton, who one hundred years ago wrote,

"Today is a pleasant day to live, a gloomy one to die."

November 26, 1975 was the day when Captain Eby looked death in the eye and death blinked first, and Thanksgiving 1975 became a pleasant day to live after all.

Near-collision of jetliners blamed on two controllers

WASHINGTON (UPI) — Safety investigators say lax performance by two radar controllers almost caused two jetliners to collide 35,000 ...

distracted, did not keep close watch and failed to point out the potentially hazardous situation to another controller who

He spotted the impending disaster 50 seconds later, in time to issue a warning.

★★★Nation
Jet controller found at fault

Scripps Wire Services

WASHINGTON—A jumbo jet from Chicago nearly smashed into another jumbo jet over Lake Erie last Nov. 26 because a distracted air traffic controller failed to warn his replacement two planes were on a collision course, a ...

Controller's Failure To Warn Nearly Caused Air Collision

AVIATION NEWS WHILE IT IS NEWS
Flight Line Times
Controller error cited in jumbo jet near-crash

II, No: 6 / 24 Pages / Two Sections — *Flight Line Times, First March, 1976.*

Controller error has been blamed in last November's near-collision of a DC-10 and L-1011 at 35,000 feet over Michigan, in which many say luck— more than anyone's skill— kept the huge airliners apart.

The near-collision occurred as American Flight 182, a DC-10-10, eastbound and climbing to emerge from the cloud tops, was told by a Cleveland Center controller to descend immediately because only a mile away in level flight on a westbound heading was Trans World Airlines Flight 37, a Lockheed 1011.

The two aircraft were closing at the rate of 850 knots. According to their altimeters, they missed by only 27 feet. A total 306 people were aboard the two planes.

Contributing to the accident was "an incomplete sector briefing during the change of controller personnel— about one minute before the accident," the board said.

Asked for his reaction to the board's report, John Leyden, president of the Professional Air Traffic Controllers Organization (PATCO), said, "I think they correctly identified the cause as a failure in the human factor," adding that the near-collision "seems directly attributable to the lack of a proper briefing."

Leyden, whose union represents controllers and often seeks to protect their interests during accident investigations, also said controllers sometimes tend to get "lulled to sleep" by depending on computerized radar equipment. He added that the

According to the cockpit and control center recordings, the radar controller was engaged in a discussion with several aircraft about the heights of the cloud tops when he recognized the conflict. He saw American 182 at 34,500 feet climbing to 37,000, while TWA 37 was three to four miles away on an opposite heading at 35,000 feet.

The controller asked American 182 its altitude, then called for a descent.

"When asked why he questioned the pilot of American 182 about his altitude before he issued a descent clearance, the controller stated that his first reaction was one of disbelief," NTSB said.

"In addition, he stated that since there might be a lag in the

According to American 182 captain, he heard the advice to descend and immediately used the autopilot vertical speed control to do so. Simultaneously he and the crew sighted the light of another aircraft dead ahead. He then applied forward pressure to the control wheel to avoid a crash, NTSB said. The American crew estimated the miss as ... feet.

However, NTSB also said the plane's cockpit recorder showed the captain remarking, "The ... he is," about one second before the controller called for a descent. "The captain can't remember the exact sequence during the short time span ...

TWENTY-TWO

With Family

1975

Cos Cob, Connecticut

We arrived at my sister's Greenwich Village apartment in the wee hours and Thanksgiving morning we drove up to Greenwich, Connecticut. While we were on the road, the FAA was meeting at LaGuardia Airport, reviewing the incident. Present were Captain Eby, First Officer David Narius, and Flight Engineer Bruce Hopkins.

We were greeted by Ted and Brenda, Lynda and Carol as we pulled up to their colonial house on a dead end street in the Cos Cob section of Greenwich. Laura, Leslie, and Laurence could hardly wait to tell their cousins what they had experienced.

And when it was turkey time, Ted herded the children to the kitchen table while the adults were seated in the dining room. The crystal and the silverware reflecting the light from the candles had a quieting effect on everyone. In the hush, I felt again what I had felt the night before and in the car, that we had experienced a miracle.

Eventually the children joined us in the dining room, leaning on our chairs or pushing for a share of one, stretching for a piece of pie and knocking someone's water glass over. When we adults talked about *the air disaster that wasn't,* we lowered our voices, now out of respect for the mystery.

It wasn't until we got home to Chicago after a visit with more family in Boston, that I realized I had forgotten to take the garbage out of the trunk of my car and deposit it in the office building dumpster.

Fortunately the weather had been cold.

TWENTY-THREE

Aftermath

2017

Oak Brook, Illinois

A few days after we arrived home, a *Time Magazine* reporter called asking if he could interview us for a story they were doing for the December 15 issue. They called the story, "Riding the Whip."

Time Magazine cover

Riding the Whip

The evening skies near Carleton, Mich., were overcast with scattered clouds as the two jumbo jets sped toward each other. TWA Flight 37, a Lockheed L-1011 with 114 people aboard, was cruising on course at 35,000 ft. from Philadelphia to Los Angeles. American Airlines Flight 182, a McDonnell Douglas DC-10 bound from Chicago to Newark with 194 passengers and crew, was climbing to an assigned altitude of 37,000 ft.

At 7:22 p.m., Air Traffic Controller Charles Hewitt at the Cleveland Air Route Traffic Control Center relieved another controller. Scarcely a minute after he came on duty, Hewitt saw an alarming sight shaping up on his big, dimly lit radar surveillance scope. The two green phosphorescent data blocks —small, illuminated groups of numbers and letters giving the altitude and heading of each flight—were moving perilously close to one another at a combined speed of 1,000 m.p.h.

Hewitt: American 182. Cleveland. What is your altitude?

Flight 182: Passing through 34.7 [34,700 ft.] at this time. We can see stars above us but we're still in the area of the clouds.

In five seconds Hewitt had discerned a collision for sure, and issued his urgent command: "American 182 descend immediately to 330 [33,000 ft.]!"

In an instant, the pilot of the American flight, traveling at 500 m.p.h., saw the blinking red and green lights of the TWA flight dead ahead of him. His view of the aircraft, he said later, "filled my whole windscreen." He plunged the wheel of his ascending DC-10 violently forward, sending the plane into a sudden 35° nosedive. He reached a recorded altitude only 47 ft. below the other aircraft's, and his tail may have come as close as 20 ft. to the TWA plane.

On board, the passengers and crew were hurled into chaos. "It was like riding the tail end of a snapping whip," said one passenger. Unbelted passengers, serving carts and dinner trays were flung into the air. "Everything went into a state of weightlessness," said John Ruffley, 51, a passenger from Summit, N.J. "Cocktail carts floated about the cabin along with people, plates, glasses and almost everything else. It was as if a mystic was at work. Then, when the plane pulled up [at 33,000 ft.], everything came crashing down."

Only one member of the TWA cockpit crew, the flight engineer, saw the lights of the American flight "descending under us," and TWA Flight 37 continued on uneventfully to Los Angeles.

When the lurch came aboard the American flight, Burt Herman, 44, a Chicago insurance executive traveling with his wife and three children, recalled: "We all had our seat belts on except Laurence. I grabbed him and held him down. There were screams and moans and stewardesses flying around. I exchanged looks with my wife—it was a knowing look in the eyes that this might be it. It seemed like an eternity."

American Flight 182 made an emergency landing at Detroit's Metropolitan Airport. There, 25 people, three of them seriously injured, were treated at a hospital. The remaining passengers continued on to Newark on another DC-10.

The near collision involved 308 "S.O.B.s," official parlance for souls on board, and had the two planes crashed it would have been the worst air collision ever. In 1971 a Japanese military plane struck an All Nippon Boeing 727 over Honshu, killing 162 people.

What went wrong over Michigan? The National Transportation Safety Board investigation may take several weeks, but preliminary findings point to some computer error, perhaps because it was fed wrong information. The Federal Aviation Administration has centers at points along the path of every flight above 18,000 feet within the Golden Triangle—the Chicago, New York, Washington area—where computers assign airspace to planes. Somehow, the computer assigned Flight 37 and Flight 182 to the same airspace at the same moment. The error was theoretically impossible, but something like it happened again last week. Two Boeing 727s—a TWA craft with 77 passengers and a United Air Lines jet with 60 passengers —were in the same flight lane approaching Chicago's O'Hare International Airport. The TWA captain spotted the danger and banked to the left, passing within 300 feet of the United plane. Again an alert individual had averted a catastrophe that a supposedly fail-safe system was intended to prevent.

Time Magazine- the Chartmaker's Inc.

My family and I rarely talked about our close encounter. Frightful things happen to all of us, and some are so traumatic that we bury them in the deep recesses of our mind. And then one day, out of a clear blue sky, there's a trigger that activates a suppressed memory.

Our trigger was the movie, *The Miracle on the Hudson.* "Sully," the captain in that event, became a big media story and later, a major motion picture. By comparison, Captain Eby garnered scant attention for his miracle over Michigan. And, to my knowledge, he received little to no additional publicity once the National Transportation Safety Board's investigation was closed. Even Guy's close friends and neighbors were unaware of the hero in their midst.

Thanks to Captain Guy Eby and a greater power, Thanksgiving eve 1975 was not our time to die. When we're lucky enough to step back from the rim of the abyss, lofty goals can seem within reach.

But why should it take a near death experience to mobilize the motivation to reach beyond one's self-imposed limitations?

It shouldn't! Because we all have within us a way of being—
a way that once understood, harmonized, and applied can help
us achieve far more than we give ourselves credit for.

From the diary of Holocaust victim Anne Frank, "Everyone
has inside of him a piece of good news. The good news is that
you don't know how great you can be. How much you can love!
What you can accomplish! And what your potential is."

After the trauma of 182, it became easier for me to move
beyond my comfort zones, eliminating those internal voices of
perceived limitations, and one by one, possibilities became re-
alities. And I accomplished more than I ever thought possible.

But I was always mindful that a good life is not about ma-
terialism. It's about being real and humble, about caring and
sharing. It's about touching the lives of others in meaningful
ways. Like what I've been doing for over 60 years in the life
insurance business.

With the gift of time, I attended my children's college graduations, walked my daughters down the aisle, became Papa
Burt to six grandchildren, and was around to say prayers at the
graves of my parents and sisters.

TWENTY-FOUR

Synchronicity

1990

San Diego, California

Fifteen years after our near-collision, I talked about our 1975 experience in a speech I gave at an insurance conference in San Diego. Following my presentation, an attendee approached me and said, "I'm an American Airlines pilot. I'm here as a guest of my lady friend."

Then he blew me away when he said, "I know your pilot, Guy Eby."

Psychoanalysts refer to it as synchronicity, an amazing coincidence infused with great meaning. I couldn't believe my ears. When I collected myself, I asked about Guy. He told me he is now retired and living in Florida.

I said, "It's fifteen years after the fact, but it's never too late for gratitude. Can you get me his address?"

"As soon as I obtain his permission, I'll call you," he answered.

When I returned to my office three days later, a message with Guy Eby's Ormond Beach, Florida address and phone number was waiting for me. I wrote to Guy, thanking him for his incredible life-saving maneuver. I told him how much the past fifteen years meant to me and my family. He wrote back:

Dear Mr. Herman:

Thanksgiving eve 1975 ... that was an experience that all of us on board flight 182 will never forget. They say that an experience is something that is happening to you that you wish would be happening to somebody else.

I found the Time article to be more accurate than the National Transportation Safety Board's findings. The bureaucracy protects itself by adjusting the facts whenever possible. A number of years after the incident, I attended a best friend's wedding and he introduced me to a guest who was the supervisor of the sector involving our flight.

I asked him why Hewitt, the controller, did not immediately give the order to descend when he saw the conflict on his altitude readout. The answer was Hewitt didn't believe it and so asked us to confirm our altitude, delaying the descent.

I sometimes think of our close encounter and wonder, was the gift to continue life given to me, or because someone on board was destined for a greater purpose in life.

Sincerely,
Guy Eby.

Several years later, I arranged a celebration of life party in Sarasota to honor our hero. I wanted him to meet the family he saved. I wanted my family to meet Guy Eby.

Guy approved the date and I reserved a private dining room at the Sarasota Hyatt and invited Guy, his wife, my family, and some friends. Two weeks prior to the event, Guy's wife reminded him that the date conflicted with a cruise they had long ago planned and regrettably could not change it. Neither could I as my arrangements were firm and the invitations extended. I had no choice but to go ahead with the party, honoring our hero in absentia.

Guy asked me to read this letter to my guests.

> *Greetings to all of you who were aboard American Airlines flight 182 on November 26, 1975. I am extremely disappointed to be unable to be with you today. It was an unexpected pleasure to be asked to join you all. The date coincided with a long ago planned cruise we are taking with friends.*
>
> *We have each been blessed by a higher power. I figure as of today we were each given an extra 10,298 days to celebrate life.*
>
> *Aren't we lucky! So celebrate well! Sorry to miss all of this. My very best to each of you. I hope to meet you some other time.*
>
> *My best regards to you all.*
> *Guy Eby*

The expression, *some other time,* can be interpreted as a polite euphemism for *unlikely.* And that's kind of how I took it. And by most measures, that would have been the end of the story.

And it was for another two decades.

And then it wasn't.

TWENTY-FIVE

Meeting

2017

Ormond Beach, Florida

It's November 2016. I was discussing my topic with the program chair for a speech I would be giving at an insurance industry conference the following November. The Guy Eby story piqued the program chair's curiosity and he asked,

"Is the pilot still living?"

"It's highly unlikely" I said. "After all, he was 57 in 1975 and it's now 41 years later. If Guy were still living he'd be pushing 100."

But over the next few days, I wondered, *what if he is still living?* Why not reach out to him? What had I to lose? And so I googled Guy Eby and found his address and a telephone listing.

After four rings, the answering machine picked up and identified the Eby residence. I had no way of knowing if the voice was Guy's and even if it was, maybe his family never got around to changing the answering machine message when he passed away? This sort of thing happens all the time. It's called a digital cemetery. The message I left for Guy went something like this:

"This is Chicago passenger Burt Herman calling Captain Guy Eby of American 182 Thanksgiving Eve 1975. If you read me, call 630-617-5- - -."

Guy did and left this message on my answering machine:

"Burt, this is Guy Eby returning your call. Anxious to talk to you and look forward to your return call."

I returned Guy's call, telling him I needed to come give him a big hug. We arranged to meet at his Ormond Beach home on February 9, 2017. Ormond Beach is a four-hour drive from my Sarasota residence.

I could hardly wait to turn the clock back. To hear directly from the pilot what really happened over 41 years ago. I could tell from our letters, phone conversations, and later on our email exchanges, how with it Guy was.

And so it came to pass that at 11 am, February 9, 2017, 15,015 days following our Thanksgiving miracle, I would knock on the front door of Guy Eby's Ormond Beach, Florida ranch house, and when he answered it, with tears welling up in our eyes, I would exclaim "Oh my gosh, it's you! It's really you. What a thrill. My hero. My hero." And it was recorded by the local media whom I had notified about the meeting.

I presented Guy with a bottle of champagne and a cake decorated with "American 182, Hero Pilot, Guy Eby, 11-26-75" and perched on top of the cake was my son's boarding pass, which he gave me when he learned I was meeting the pilot. I had no idea he kept it all those years.

Danish philosopher, Soren Kierkegaard said, "Life can

only be understood looking backward, but must be lived going forward."

Several reporters and I spent the next four hours looking back with Guy Eby. When a reporter asked Guy what he thought about my visit, he said, "It was very nice that Herman came to see me today and share his story from the other side of the plane, which I had never heard before."

And I said, "It was hard to believe it was happening after all this time."

So after half a lifetime, Guy's long overdue recognition and my gratitude converged and was dramatically reported on the front page of the February 11, 2017 *Daytona Beach News Journal* with this headline: HIGH ALTITUDE GRATITUDE.

We had more copy that day than President Trump's immigration story.

NEWS-JOURNAL

HOME OF THE WORLD'S MOST FAMOUS BEACH | Volusia Edition

Saturday, February 11, 2017

News-Journalonline.com $1   **f** daytonabeachnewsjournal   **🐦** @thenwnjournal

PRESIDENT'S TRAVEL BAN

Trump considers new order

By Matt Zapotosky, Philip Rucker and Rachel Weiner
The Washington Post

Trump

WASHINGTON — President Donald Trump said Friday that he is considering rewriting his executive order temporarily barring refugees and citizens of seven Muslim-majority countries from entering the country, indicating that the administration may try to quickly restore some aspects of the now-frozen travel ban or replace it with other face-saving measures.

Trump told reporters aboard Air Force One that he would probably wait until Monday or Tuesday to take any action, and White House Chief of Staff Reince Priebus said several options — including taking the case to the Supreme Court — were still on the table.

Trump hinted that the ongoing legal wrangling might move too slowly for his taste, though he thought he would ultimately prevail in court.

"We will win that battle," he said. "The unfortunate part is that it takes time statutorily, but we will win that battle. We also have a lot of other options,

including just filing a brand-new order."

He said among the revisions he might make are "new security measures."

A three-judge panel of the U.S. Court of Appeals for the 9th Circuit ruled unanimously

SEE ORDER, A13

REUNION IN ORMOND BEACH

HIGH-ALTITUDE GRATITUDE

Passenger in near-miss thanks pilot after 41 years

Retired pilot Guy Eby gets a big hug from Burt Herman 41 years after Herman says Eby saved his and others' lives. The two men met at Herman's insistence Thursday at Eby's Ormond Beach home. (NEWS-JOURNAL/DAVID TUCKER)

By Tony Holt
tony.holt@news-jrnl.com

ORMOND BEACH — The choppy air above southwest Michigan was a nuisance, so the pilot decided to fly higher.

Visibility was reduced to nothing due to cloud cover, but Guy Eby hoped it would make the Nov. 26, 1975, evening flight to Newark smoother. He got the OK from the control tower and he made his climb toward 37,000 feet.

Eby didn't know it yet, but he was

seconds from potential doom. The tower in Cleveland was going through a shift change, so a new air-traffic controller was taking his seat and needed a few moments to fully absorb what he was seeing on his screen. TWA Flight 37 was cruising west. Eby's American Airlines Flight 182 was heading east. Its altitude was slightly lower, but its upward trajectory was moving directly into the path of the TWA flight.

Then Eby saw the TWA L-1011. "There he is," he said.

Emotional moment

 Watch a video and see more photos from the heartfelt reunion:
news-journalonline.com

Eby pushed his control stick forward for a sudden descent.
The jet dropped.

SEE REUNION, A16

WEST VOLUSIA PLANS

Automall proposed near DeLand

By Dustin Wyatt
dustin.wyatt@news-jrnl.com

DELAND — A proposed automall for Orange Camp Road has revved up complaints.

Brendan Hurley, owner of Hurley Chrysler Jeep Dodge, wants to move his business from South Woodland Boulevard to a 20-acre plot between the sprawling Victoria Park development and Interstate 4, just outside the DeLand city limits. The plan, which would include a cluster of dealerships, will be voted on Tuesday in a public meeting by the Volusia County Planning and Land Development Regulation Commission. The County Council would then have the final say March 16.

Hurley did not return a call to his business Friday.

Ahead of Tuesday's vote, DeLand city officials and county council members say they've been inundated with emails from residents of Victoria Park and surrounding neighborhoods who are opposed to the plan.

But a small sliver of the property sits in the city of Lake Helen and Vice Mayor Vernon Burton said he hasn't seen the same resistance there.

"I am not opposed to it until I know more about it," he said, adding that the possibility of new development in city limits sounds promising. "As it is right now, the idea does have a nice ring to it."

A16 Saturday, February 11, 2017 | The Daytona Beach News-Journal

REUNION
Continued from A1

Had Eby's reaction been 0.01 second slower, there would have been a collision – catastrophe at 35,000 feet.

It would have been the worst aircraft-against-aircraft disaster in U.S. aviation history – a death total exceeding 300 people one day before Thanksgiving. The American flight's vertical stabilizer, which serves as the plane's rudder, missed scraping the bottom of the TWA aircraft by roughly 10 feet.

Even all these years later, Eby believes it was the closest two civilian planes have ever come to crashing into each other in the sky.

Now 96, Eby had never met any of his passengers from that night – until this week. But Herman, one of the 182 on board the McDonnell Douglas DC-10, drove from his Sarasota vacation home to Eby's Ormond Beach house, stood on his front porch and knocked on the door.

Eby doesn't move fast these days, but when he heard that knock on Thursday, he showed vigor when he got off the sofa to get the door.

The long-awaited reunion was predictably an emotional one.

"Oh my gosh. Oh my gosh. It's you," Herman said as he set his briefcase on the floor and moved in for a hug. "What a thrill. My hero. My hero."

That was what Herman vowed to do the moment he saw Eby – give his hero a hug. When Eby offered his hand, Herman extended his arms for an embrace.

Tears streamed down Eby's cheeks.

Hollywood worthy

Herman's wife Elaine, his twin daughters Laura and Leslie and son Larry were with him on the flight.

For decades, Herman says he has mentioned Eby, the pilot, during prayers at the Thanksgiving table.

Eby is every bit the hero as Chesley Sullenberger, who executed an emergency landing eight years ago on the Hudson River, saving the lives of 155 people, Herman contends. Unlike the American-TWA near-crash, the "Miracle on the Hudson" was filmed and aired on news stations across the world, and later depicted in a major motion picture. By comparison, Eby's heroism garnered little attention aside from a few wire stories and a short article in Time magazine.

"He deserves a movie," Herman said. "If they can make a movie about Sully, they need to make a movie about Guy Eby."

American Airlines issued no commendation or medal. Eby said his chief pilot at the time preferred not to publicize

Burt Herman holds a photograph of his family as he visits with Guy Eby, at left, Thursday at Eby's Ormond Beach home. Eby piloted an American Airlines flight in 1975 on which Herman, his wife, daughters and son were passengers, and which came within feet of a midair collision with a TWA passenger jet over Michigan. Herman credits Eby's quick reaction, diving the American jet 1,000 feet, missing the other plane and saving the lives of all aboard both flights. [NEWS-JOURNAL/DAVID TUCKER]

NEAR MISS

A Time magazine diagram shows how close the American Airlines DC-10 that Guy Eby was piloting and a TWA L-1011 came to a midair collision on Nov. 28, 1975. [NEWS-JOURNAL/DAVID TUCKER]

Newspaper clippings from 1975 detail the near miss between an American Airlines DC-10 and a TWA L-1011 due to a controllers mistake. [NEWS-JOURNAL/DAVID TUCKER]

through letters in 1991. A reunion of passengers on that flight was scheduled years ago, but Eby couldn't attend.

Herman finally arranged to meet Eby on Thursday.

While together, Herman was overflowing with words and gestures of appreciation. His wife couldn't join him on the cross-state drive, but he handed Eby the phone so he could hear her thank him for saving her life. He got his twin daughters on the phone so they could do the same.

When they wandered into the kitchen, Herman took out a photograph of his family. His son Larry is a former tax lawyer who now runs the family business, the Herman Agency.

Leslie is a certified public accountant who works for her brother's company. His other daughter, Laura, used

night over Michigan. Eby compared his visibility to driving through a dense fog on a rural road at night.

Almost none.

Over the radio the TWA pilot, who was flying from Philadelphia to Los Angeles, discussed his flight conditions.

His description of the cloud cover matched perfectly with what Eby was seeing through his windscreen.

"I wonder where he is," Eby said.

A glow of light through the clouds caught his attention. He realized it was coming from a cabin of an approaching plane. Two commercial jets carrying a combined 308 people were careening nose-to-nose at a closing rate of 1,000 mph, according to news reports at the time.

By the time the panicked air-traffic controller, who had just

the incident, one passenger described it as "like riding the tail end of a snapping whip."

Herman has a vivid memory of that experience. He recalled serving carts, glasses, plates, cigarette butts and flight attendants floating in mid-air. His son Larry was among those not wearing a seatbelt. Yet Herman couldn't defy physics. Larry banged against the overhead compartment, but wasn't hurt.

When altitude was maintained and gravity was restored, everything came crashing down. Herman's clothes were stained with coffee. Liquor, and other drinks. All liquids on the plane, including what was inside the bathrooms, splashed against the floor and seeped into the carpet lining the fuselage.

Inside the TWA cock-

on that flight met with representatives from the Federal Aviation Administration, who conducted interviews. Eby recalled one flight attendant running to him, wrapping her arms around him and kissing him squarely on the lips.

"Thank you for saving my life," she told him.

A hero once before

Eby was the last to exit the plane. When he stepped out of the cockpit and scanned the vacant cabin, he saw red splotches on the ceiling. In that moment he was horrified. He thought he was seeing blood. He knew there were injured passengers, some of whom had to be removed from the plane on stretchers. He soon realized that lasagna had been served. The stains were tomato sauce.

There were 24 injuries reported on Eby's flight, including three who were seriously injured, but everyone survived, according to the incident report. It was the second

a job with American Airlines in 1959 and retired after 28 years. He was married three times.

His third wife, Ruth, "kept" Eby, "the best of the three," he said, died in 2015.

Today, the 96-year-old retired pilot uses a hearing aid, but his memory remains sharp, and he moves around his house with ease. He still drives his red Infiniti convertible, which he showed off to Herman during his visit.

Even still, Eby has lived with one lingering doubt.

After the pilot pulled out of the descent and established a steady altitude toward Detroit, Eby got on the intercom and assured passengers that the aircraft was structurally sound and notified them about the pending emergency landing. That was the last thing he said to the passengers.

He said nothing about the near collision. Now from the cabin he the vantage point to see the aircraft that nearly

Later that day, Guy sent me this email: "When I picked up the paper, I looked for the article in the center section. I found it, but trying to read it, I was surprised to discover it was continued from the front page. I was shocked. I racked back to find our picture on the front page and in color. Since I never told any of our friends about our experience, I had many phone calls today.

Over the following weeks our meeting was reported in many Florida newspapers, the *Chicago Tribune* and the Tribune's Pioneer Press publications, the *Oak Brook* and *Hinsdale Doings*.

The 2/16/17 *Sarasota Florida Observer* article began with these words:

"Burt Herman and Guy Eby didn't meet until last week, but in 1975 they came close to dying together. Their meeting that day was the first time the pair had met face to face."

Seeing "close to dying together" in print, took my breath away all over again.

On March 9, 2017 the *Chicago Tribune* ran the story of our meeting with this headline:

AFTER 41 YEARS, MAN MEETS, THANKS PILOT

Saying our good-byes at the end of a remarkable day, Guy asked if he should have told the passengers the reason for the plunge. I thought for a minute and responded, "I don't think so. If we knew, we wouldn't have slept much that night. There was just too much to get over at the time."

He said, "That was something I wanted to hear for a long time."

Guy's step-daughter Penney Peirce, who lives near Guy in Ormond Beach, joined us for the reunion. Penney is a well-known intuitive counselor, popular international speaker, and author on the subjects of intuition, higher perception, and sensitivity development. Who better to sum up Guy's reaction to the happening, than Penney. The next day she sent me this email:

> Burt, thanks so much for facilitating this event. I know it meant a huge amount to Guy who is a man of few words. I think after it was over, it really registered. I told him he erased all his karma from all his lives with those acts of heroism.
>
> After my mom died, he has been very heroic as well. I know he is lonely but keeps his sense of humor, his wits, friends and projects. And I'm glad he decided to adopt a dog. She has been perfect with her happy nature.
>
> Many Blessings,
> Penney

Penney and Guy

TWENTY-SIX

Guy's Sons

2017

Florida / Chicago

After the war, Guy flew in the Berlin Airlift, and in 1950 became a pilot for American Airlines, retiring 28 years later, in 1978, at age 60.

Guy's sons, Robert and Wayne.

When asked what he remembered about the near miss of '75, Wayne said, "Thank goodness, Dad was the pilot."

"Why is that?" I asked, hoping he would elaborate, tell me a story.

"Because Dad was paying attention. He never lost his focus, and never got thrown by the unexpected.

"When I was still a kid at home," he went on. "I went up in his Swift with him and was flying the plane when he pulled back all the power and said to me, 'Where are you going to land?' He taught us that in a single engine plane you always have to know where you are going to land."

"As a boy," Wayne said, "I hoped to be a pilot, but I had trouble all my young life with ear infections and had to give up that dream." Not through singing his dad's praises, Wayne said, "Dad was prepared for anything to happen—he was a great pilot."

I asked his older brother, Robert, why he thought his dad had been able to avert the TWA jumbo jet and save all those lives, and his answer was, "Dad was extremely thorough. He knew every nut and bolt, every system and held how it worked in his head. He thought far, far ahead of the airplane," Robert added, and as a pilot, he said that he had learned from his father to do the same.

"And what motivated him to do that?" I asked.

"To be one step ahead always. He took his job seriously. A lot of the guys don't. They're too casual about it all—act sometimes like it's a party. I see that attitude all the time," Robert added.

But Wayne had the story to tell.

"No one ever knew this, but Dad's copilot on the 182 flight was reading a magazine during the preflight instrument check-in at O'Hare, and Dad told him to cut it out, put the magazine down. They were taxiing out onto the runway and the copilot was still poring over the magazine, so Dad reached across and grabbed it out his copilot's hands and stuffed it into his ready bag. I imagine he had something to say, but he didn't tell me that. Dad is easy-going, never makes a fuss about things as long as you're doing your job."

Wayne mentioned he had helped his dad modify his Swift and I was reminded of his father's story about working on cars in Clyde's garage as a teenager. "Where did you work on the Swift?" I asked, picturing Guy under a car in Clyde's garage in Hershey.

"A little airstrip in Madison, Connecticut, called Griswold's where Dad kept his plane."

"In a hangar?" I asked.

"I guess you could call it that since that's where the small planes hung out. It was just a building with a higher than usual ceiling and large doors. Pretty rough. Walls and floor gray except where paint had been spilled and grease ground in. We brought our own tools in a tool box that sat on the asphalt next to the plane with a bucket of rags, touch-up paint, and numerals that had a black tacky self-stick glue on them. They were always getting stuck to the rags in the bucket. We weren't the neatest guys."

"So what sorts of things did you do to the plane?" I asked.

"The time I most remember we put some new covers on the landing gear. We were down on our knees on a towel on the asphalt, when Griswold came walking in with a beer and a big smile. He had a story to tell Dad who paid him no attention at all. I don't think Dad spoke a word to him, which I thought was strange, so when Griswold gave up and walked away, I asked Dad, "What was that?"

Dad pulled himself up off the asphalt and told me that Griswold had killed a girl.

"There were two landing lanes, an asphalt one and an old, unused grass one," Dad said. "Griswold brought a girl to the strip one afternoon to impress her. Took her up and after buzzing around, decided to try a landing on the grass. It was in bad shape and the plane crash-landed, tipping over, crushing the girl. Griswold didn't have a scratch."

"That's some story," I said unable to think of anything better to say.

"That's how Dad was. He never spoke to Griswold after that and it wasn't long before Dad moved his plane out."

I asked, "So how did you help him?"

Wayne smiled and said, "I handed Dad the tools."

When Robert was 14, he accompanied his dad on the delivery of a Beechcraft B55 Baron to Lake Maggiore, a long thin island on the south side of the Alps that is shared by Italy and Switzerland.

I asked Robert why he and not his brother, Wayne, had been selected to make the trip. His answer was that Wayne didn't show the interest he did and was two years younger. Robert then told me the story of his adventure.

"Dad and I took off from MacArthur Islip Airport the summer of '64. The Barron had six seats with green plaid fabric upholstery. We folded up the two rows of two seats each to make room for two 55-gallon fuel drums we needed in order to have

Robert & Guy in front of Beach Baron

the range for the trans-Atlantic flight. The folded chairs were tucked behind the fuel drums and our water raft was lying on top of them.

"We were headed for Gander, Newfoundland, Canada. Our route was almost the same route that Charles Lindbergh took to Paris many years before. Dad had been to Gander numerous times in the navy during the Berlin Airlift, flying a Douglas C-54 Skymaster. Dad flew that first leg of our journey, but I would have my hours.

"We could hear each other over the exterior noise, but it wasn't conducive to small talk. Dad would tell me what he was doing and why and when I took over he'd tell me what to do and why. I learned a lot about flying on that trip. Looking back, it was a rare privilege to have the instructor I had at 14 years old.

"The airport at Gander was larger than the one in the Azores and in Nice, but nearly empty because of the recent innovations in engines and fuel that made far fewer fuel stops along a journey necessary. It was disappointing to see beautiful airport terminals nearly abandoned. However, because of the lack of traffic, we could taxi right up to the terminal. The exception was in Nice, where we had to park with the small planes a mile down the airport and carry our luggage.

"We spent the night in Gander at a hunting lodge with 12 other parties. We could hear the caribou in the night 'calling out for romance,' Dad explained, although I knew about such things. Maybe Dad just liked to acknowledge it. He was a bit of a lady's man. Not ever embarrassingly so, but he had an eye on women and I think they found him appealing. Heck, at 98 he drives a red convertible."

"After spending the night in Gander and finding a start cart to start the Baron, we took off for the Azores. For some reason, we found our battery dead that morning, which led Dad to telling me a story about flying in the Berlin airlift after the war.

Guy's convertible

"One day his engine wouldn't start so he unloaded his passengers and ran the plane on three engines until the wind going through the propeller got that fourth engine going. With all four engines working, he could fly back and pick up his load of passengers.

"If Dad hadn't told me that story I would have been out of luck ten years later in the Bahamas, flying a charter for Florida National Airways. I wouldn't have known what to do when one of my engines wouldn't start.

"When we landed in the Azores, we were treated like kings, as Barons ourselves. Seven or eight or possibly as many as ten people came running to greet our plane and shake our hands. We were living for a moment in Lindberg's skin. That night I had the best meal I've ever had, seven courses that included everything that archipelago in the middle of the Atlantic could offer.

"The Azores were a surprise to me. Who would have ever expected such dramatic landscapes and green pastures in the middle of the ocean with hedgerows of blue hydrangeas.

"The next morning we had a very thorough briefing from the meteorologist for the weather along the next leg, Azores to Nice, France, over Portugal and Spain. That happened to be the longest leg of our flight a little over nine hours and I flew most of it.

"Every time I'm asked what it's been like being Guy Eby's son, I say that it's like living with high expectations on me. I always felt strong because my dad saw me strong. I always felt I could do whatever was needed, because he expected that of me.

"We ran into thunderstorms on the next leg, from the

Azores over Portugal and Spain to Nice in France. This made me think of the lyrics from *My Fair Lady* ... "The rain in Spain stays mainly in the plain." It was another opportunity to watch my dad at work, this time hopping in and out of storm clouds. He had a good time. Meanwhile I was small enough to crawl back and check the fuel drums. I had to open the valves now and again to equalize pressure and keep the plane stable.

"Then it was two days in beautiful Nice with its white buildings and red flowers and a walk on the French Riviera, which was a surprise like the Azores. I was expecting a stroll on a sandy beach but the Riviera's shoreline is mainly rock formation and stones. We stayed in the Carlton Cannes hotel that was used in the Cary Grant film *To Catch a Thief* with Grace Kelly."

His descriptions brought back fond memories of my 21 months on active naval reserve duty in French Morocco and the trip I took to Monaco at the time of Grace Kelly's wedding on April 19, 1956.

"Those days were followed by a four-hour flight to Milan, Italy, where we met up with the client for the Baron and stayed in the hotel famous for being where Mussolini's body hung out front. In the back there was a garden with an outdoor movie theater playing Italian movies all night. Dad and I, with a window on the garden, could have stayed up all night watching movies, but the next morning after a meeting, we had to climb back into the Baron for the delivery flight.

"We flew out of Milan, then up Lake Maggiore with the Alps towering around us. I don't know which was scarier, driving the three-lane roads in Milan where the middle lane was for passing cars coming in either direction or flying at low altitude from 3,000 feet down to 1,500 feet, through the Alps to get the best view of the lake and the valley for Dad who was behind a movie camera while I was at the controls. It was the most remarkable sight I'd ever seen, but I was only 14. After fifty years of travel it is still the most remarkable sight I have seen, the immense stone walls nature built with snowy tips that we had to look up to see.

"At the far end of the lake, we landed on a grass field that was the Aeroporto Cantonale di Locarno of Switzerland. There was a phone hanging from a small office building that we used to call for a customs official. After waiting sometime for the Swiss Custom Agent to arrive, we finally saw in the distance, approaching on a bicycle, a man wearing a fine-looking gray uniform.

"He got off the black bicycle notable because it was polished to a high shine, removed a rubber stamp and ink pad from a wooden box on the back of the bicycle, took our passports and used the same box as a little table to process our passports, then handed them back to us and peddled off down the grass strip.

"While waiting for the client who was driving up from Milan, we removed the fuel drums and re-installed the four rear passenger seats and cleaned up the Baron so she looked brand new.

"The way back, we drove down the east side of the famous Lake Como with its terra cotta, butter, and blush villas, dripping with fascia that dotted the perimeter of the deep emerald green lake.

"It was such remarkable sights: the architecture of the old

world, the winding roads dressed with red flowers, the bright casino and of course the majestic Alps. But what stirred me most was the flying. I am my father's son."

Today, his father, the 99-year-old retired pilot uses a hearing aid, but his memory remains sharp, and he moves around his house with ease. He also drives a large Lexus in which he took me and step-daughter Penney to lunch after the reporters left.

Guy retired from American on November 8, 1978 after completing his last flight from Bermuda to Boston. It was to my hometown on my 47th birthday. A situational irony foreshowing a serendipitous meeting 37 years later.

This was the teletype Guy was handed when he landed.

```
#
QD BOSDIAA
.HDQNYAA 071614
BOSDIAA RESTUCCIA CPY NYCDIAA WETHERBEE
PLEASE HOLD FOR ARRIVAL OF CAPTAIN GUY EBY OFF FLIGHT 614
FROM BERMUDA ARRIVING BOSTON 1622 ON 8 TH NOVEMBER.
GUY CONGRATULATIONS AND BEST WISHES ON YOUR RETIREMENT FROM
AMERICAN. YOUR 28 YEARS OF DEDICATION AND PROFESSIONAL
ATTITUDE IS RECOGNIZED AND APPRECIATED BY ALL OF US. THE BEST OF
HEALTH AND HAPPINESS TO YOU AND YOURS DURING YOUR RETIREMENT.

DONALD J. LLOYD-JONES SENIOR VICE PRESIDENT-OPERATIONS
①
071626
ACN 373
```

Guy's final flight

The crew decorated the cabin.

While Guy retired from American at the age of 60, and his calling card says Captain Retired, Guy did not retire from life. Far from it. It's now 39 years post-retirement and Guy is still going strong.

TWENTY-SEVEN

Other Voices

December 16, 2017

Thirty years after WWII, Guy received this amazing letter from the plane captain of the seaplane he had rescued over the East China Sea:

> Guy:
>
> According to local newspapers, a Capt C.A. Eby of American had a "near miss" near Detroit. It must have been a misprint because I don't believe there could be two Eby's that would have the thoughtfulness and cool to perform such evasive measures so quickly and avert a disaster.
>
> The passengers on that plane and the #3 crew of VPB-27 owe you a great debt of gratitude for your performance.
>
> That day back in '45 is a day I will never forget. Thanks again.
>
> If you ever set down in Detroit for a few hours, I'd appreciate a call, and if time allows I would come up and see you. It would be a pleasure.
>
> the old plane cap't
> C J or "Pop"

The Chairman of Lloyds Bank of California who was a passenger on TWA 37 sent this letter of gratitude to Al Casey of American Airlines:

Dear Sir:

I am deeply indebted to Captain Guy Eby for his expert performance. By coincidence I met Guy Eby at a friend's daughter's wedding some three or four years ago. He is a delightful person and I would be happy to meet him again someday. But I am also delighted we did not meet 34,700 feet over Detroit on Thanksgiving eve. By this letter I wish to commend Guy Eby and would appreciate your passing this message on to him.

And this was American's response to 182 passenger, Harry Pilitsis.

Dear Mr. Pilitsis:

Trying is a mild word for what you went through on November 26th. The superb action of Captain Guy Eby and his crew is a magnificent example of airmanship skill and cause for pride and gratitude. You are a thoughtful man and I will have the pleasure of sending your commendations to Captain Eby and all of the crew members.

Albert Casey

American Airlines

Chicago Tribune reporter, Chuck Fieldman forwarded this email to me.

Hal Savage

My name is Hal Savage and I reside in Long Beach Township, New Jersey. I recently saw your article from the good 'ole **Chicago Tribune** *on the internet and a corresponding article in the* **Daytona Beach News Journal** *about a man named Burt Herman. He was a passenger on Flight 182 American Airlines out of O'Hare to Newark, N.J. on November 26, 1975, when a collision almost took place over Lake Michigan, had it not been for the split-second timing of Captain Eby. I too was a passenger on that flight and for years have been wondering and trying to find anybody who was on it and moreover, who the Captain was, to extend my thanks to him and his crew for saving my life. At the time, I was a law student at Lewis University in Glen Ellyn, Illinois.*

As I recall it was one of those snowy cold days in Illinois. I had just finished up classes that morning and went to pack and hurry to the airport. The flight was scheduled to leave at 4:40 pm. 182 was coming from San Francisco and was on time, but when it landed at O'Hare mechanical problems seems to ensue and the flight was delayed in taking off until 6 pm.

I was seated in the second row of the plane, seat 2 H. One of the stewardesses came around and gave me a Michelob beer and by the time we were ready to taxi out she collected glasses. I recall we waited in line for takeoff. I took out a torts case book and started reading. The book remained on my lap as we were climbing and I heard the power of the aircraft as it went up. Then came that kind of quiet when you heard the pilots level off and feather back the engines until they power up to climb again. The stewardess came around again with the drink service and handed me a new glass and the bottle of beer. I remember placing the glass in the console area between seats and pouring the liquid into the glass. I took one drink of the beer and remember feeling the climb of the aircraft again. The seat belt sign was still on and I was still reading the book on my lap. At this point I wanted to go to the bathroom and I unbuckled my seat belt. The aircraft was leveling off again, so I thought I had a few minutes. I took one more swig of beer and that's when everything went wild. I never made it to the bathroom.

Before I could get the glass to my lips, the beer in the glass climbed right up and out of the glass. My right hand and arm began to rise and before I knew it, I was crashing into the ceiling of the plane directly above my seat.

It happened so fast that when I hit the ceiling, I don't even recall hitting it. It was surreal. I landed back down in what I remember was the aisle of the plane and tried to get my senses about me. The man who was sitting next to me was covered in beer that had flown out of my glass. We looked at each other in utter disbelief. A creepy feeling came over me and I started thinking, I could die tonight. There were screams and cries throughout the plane. Across the aisles people were hovering over seat 2A and 2B where a stewardess lay bleeding. At this time the flight deck door opened and the 1st officer and the flight engineer walked through the cabin and looked at the devastation. They were talking in low voices, but I distinctly heard the one man say to the other, "We were so close I could see the faces of the crew on the other plane."

The captain came on the intercom and told us that the aircraft was structurally sound and we would be landing in Detroit shortly."

During that emotionally charged day with Guy, my wife, Elaine, and three children called Guy to express their gratitude.

Elaine's words:

"Sitting next to my daughters, across the aisle from my husband and son, I was speechless. I didn't want to believe what I was seeing and hearing: bodies flying around the cabin, my son catapulted to the overhead bin, screaming passengers. My husband and I exchanged looks. Knowing looks that this might be it. I knew it was more than wind shear or an air pocket or turbulence of some sort. Not when the aircraft is nose down. Not with weightlessness. Not with the toilets backing up. No, this was something much worse. Really bad. Then seconds later we leveled off and minutes later we landed and thanks to you, our lives began anew."

When I asked about his recollections, my son Larry said, "I vividly recall a stewardess lying in the aisle, bleeding profusely from a head wound and how we applied first aid with makeshift bandages."

Remember Marla, the 20-year-old Northwestern University student? The one who fell asleep soon after takeoff, then went flying. Well, even though her name had changed through marriage, I located her living in Upper Saddle River, New Jersey. We had a stirring telephone conversation. I told her I remember seeing a young woman hit the ceiling, landing in the aisle near us. I recall the paramedics immobilizing and removing her by stretcher. We agreed it must have been her.

Marla told me that her injuries resulted in significant life changes, like no longer being able to travel from New Jersey to Evanston. She said she had to transfer to a college closer to home and she changed her major. And how flight 182 ultimately resulted in a great outcome for her life. The once upon a time 20-year-old Northwestern University student is now the 62-year-old, forever grateful, wife of Frank Walter, mother of Samantha and Zachary, and a successful businesswoman.

The following day she sent me this email:

It was incredibly emotional connecting with you yesterday. I was so moved by all that you had done to connect with this very special man who saved so many lives.

Frank and Marla with children Samatha and Zachery

Thanks to *Chicago Tribune* reporter Chuck Fieldman for helping me find flight 182 passenger Mary Florence Brady, age 93, formerly of La Grange, Illinois, now living in a retirement home in Denver, Colorado. All we had to go on was a Mrs. William Brady. That was some good detective work.

I left Mary a voice mail message. When she returned my call the first thing she said was, "I thought your call might be a scam."

When Mary was satisfied I was legit, she said, "The timing of your

Mary Brady

phone call was unbelievable as I had recently shared our flight 182 story with some friends for the first time. Over the years, I couldn't really talk about it. And then your awesome call came a few days later!"

Mary continued. "My family, six of us, were on flight 182, including my father who was in his 80's. My husband, son and two daughters—my son passed away five years ago. We were traveling to New Jersey to visit my daughter Mary Beth and her husband. When I told my boss that I was nervous about all of us flying together, he said, "All you have to be concerned about are takeoffs and landings." He neglected to tell me about the middle.

"My husband Bill flew up to the ceiling and landed back down on his seat. A serving cart fell on his hand badly cutting it. My son's turtleneck shirt and hair were covered with cottage cheese. When my eldest daughter Mary Beth, who was waiting for us at the Newark airport first saw her brother she said, "At least you could have worn a clean shirt. She was told the reason for our delay was due to an illness on the plane and she assumed it was her grandfather.

"When my husband, Bill, used the restroom at the Detroit airport, he overheard two men claiming it was a near miss. 'Oh, Dad, that's ridiculous!' My daughter Therese said.

We rarely talked about our experience. Even my husband, a World War II veteran, couldn't talk about it. Bill passed away eleven years ago.

"Our return flight to O'Hare was a rough one due to the stormy weather. We were stacked up. I recall we circled for a long time.

"I'm very grateful for my life. I was an only child but I had four children, ten grandchildren, and I'm expecting my

Brady Family photo - 50ᵗʰ Wedding Anniversary

9th, 10th, and 11th great-grandchildren this year.

"It's still hard to imagine how close we came to dying. Thank God for a good pilot."

Mary Beth's first husband passed away and she is married to Joseph Bright, a tax attorney. Mary Beth's son is a Northwestern and Kellogg grad.

I told Mary Brady that my grandson is a Northwestern freshman and my son and son-in law are Northwestern Law School grads and there was at least one other Northwestern student on our flight. I shared this with the *Northwestern Alumni* magazine hoping they'll do a flight 182/Northwestern connection story.

On August 26, 2017, Paula Peirce, the pilot's step-daughter, visited Mary Brady at her Denver retirement home.

How special was that!

Paula sent me this email.

*We had a delightful visit with Mary Brady. She is cer-
tainly an energetic woman with a passion for life. She
talked about many of the things you already had mentioned to Penney and Guy." She said, "The passengers
did not know what was happening when the plane went
up slightly and then dove suddenly. It's odd the things
you remember and the images that stay in your mind.
I remember my husband had his seat belt off getting
ready to pay for a drink when the dinner cart arrived.
He was thrown up to the ceiling and broke the ceiling
tiles before he landed back on his seat. The serving cart
also flew into the air and landed on top of him cutting his hand. Food and glassware had flown to the
ceiling as well and broken glass fell into my husband's
hair. My family thought they were going to die. We were
transported to the hospital to be checked out. When we
returned to the airport, we were asked not to say too
much about what had happened."*

Mary is quick to remember that her entire family was
on that flight except the daughter they were visiting in New
Jersey. If anything had happened on that flight, Mary's
daughter would now be alone. Mary shared photos of many
family celebrations over the years … weddings, birthdays,
family holidays. This large, very close Brady family has enjoyed a lifetime of memories and experiences together. All of

which would have been cut short if not for that heroic day.

A few days after Paula's visit, Mary Brady called Guy Eby. Then she called me to share her euphoria about finally connecting with the pilot.

The following day, Guy sent me this email:

I thought Mary was a delightful person, very much like my third wife, "Skip." We spoke for more than a half hour.

You just can't make this stuff up.

With that, I had the segue I needed to ask Guy about his three wives. And he was very forthcoming.

He began, "After World War II, following instrument flight instructors school in Atlanta, I was assigned to the VR-7 which was located in Opa Locka, Florida. The squadron flew the DC-3 to the Panama Canal and Trinidad. It was here that I met Barbara Nelson in Hollywood, Florida. Barbara would later become my first wife. My squadron was decommissioned in July 1945 and I was reassigned to the VR 3 at Patuxent River, Maryland. I drove to my parent's home in Carlisle and spent five days there before going to my new base at Patuxent River.

"While in Carlisle, I called Vivian and Voni Watson, my old girlfriends. Carlisle was home to an army base for indotrination of doctors, dentists and veterinarians. Voni worked at the Post Exchange and came in contact with many officers. So she and her sister were booked up weeks in advance. Both were very busy when I tried to date either one.

"I called Barbara who lived in Sea Cliff, Long Island.

She invited me to Sea Cliff, which was a six-hour drive from Carlisle. Later she would come to Washington and we would drive to the base at Patuxent River. I had a friend on the base who was in my old squadron and Barbara would stay with them. She also came to Carlisle and spent time in my parent's home. Carlisle's entertainment center and mixer was at the Molly Pitcher where the patrons danced to live organ music. It was here that Barbara met Voni.

"On my last date with Voni, I told her that I was engaged to Barbara.

Her response was, "Why didn't you ask me?"

Barbara and I were married on March 4, 1947 at the Chapel at the air station. I was one of many Naval reservists who were discharged during a cutback of service personnel. After several months, I heard that American Airlines was recruiting pilots. I was hired as a flight engineer before upgrading to copilot and later I became a Convair 240 Captain. During my American career I was always based in New York, except for the initial few months in Memphis as a flight engineer. I was upgraded to DC-6 and DC-7 and years later to Lockheed Electra and then Convair 990 and Boeing 707 and then the DC-10.

"I was living in Madison, Connecticut until my retirement. It took five years to sell our Connecticut home. We looked for home sites on or near airports and decided to settle in Ormond Beach, Florida."

"Barbara developed cirrhosis. She was hospitalized for six weeks but didn't heed her doctor's advice and passed away on January 31, 1993."

"By this time, Voni was single again. She visited the area for a week before returning home to Carlisle. I saw her a few times a year and then in 1994, she told me she had cancer and would I take her in if she came to Florida? I agreed and she came in July 1994 and we were married that September. Voni also had rheumatoid arthritis and had two hip replacements. She seemed to be in constant pain. One night she overdosed on pain medication and passed away during the night of January 29, 1995."

"Skip was Barbara's best friend and lived a stone's throw from our house. I had theater tickets, which after Voni's passing, I offered to a friend who suggested I take Skip. I called her and we saw two shows; Will Rogers Follies and Rita Moreno. I always liked Skip and knew her from the times she visited Barbara. After the shows we had several dinner dates and it wasn't long before she was sleeping over. Skip had bought a house in the Trails after separating from her husband. We were married on June 26, 2002."

"And that summer I bought a Chrysler van and we drove to Oregon and down the West Coast to San Diego. Returning home, we stopped in Denver and saw Skip's daughter Paula, her husband and their two daughters, Val and Julia. Then during the winter of '96, I bought a Century Coach motor home. We went to Nova Scotia the first year. The ten years we owned it, we traveled extensively in Canada, to most of the northern US and even made one trip to Alaska. Eventually I had to sell the motor home as I was unable to maintain it for physical reasons. So see the world before your back and feet give out."

"Tell me about Skip?" I asked.

Guy said, "Skip was an accomplished writer, artist, and interior designer and one of the founding members of the Ormond Beach Art Guild and the 2015 recipient of the Guild's Lifetime Member Award. She passed away two years ago."

He added, "Skip was the best of the three."

The day after my initial phone conversation with Mary Brady, she emailed me saying that her daughter, Kathleen Staff of Carbondale, Illinois, would like to talk to me.

I called.

Kathy told me that in 1975 she was a sophomore at Southern Illinois University. That she and her family learned the terrifying details of their near miss watching TV at her sister's house in New Jersey that Thanksgiving weekend. Like everyone else, she was shocked to learn how close they came to dying.

She said, "I always wanted to thank the pilot and now I can."

Kathy married Michael Staff whom she had met a month prior to AA 182. The Staffs have two children and six grand-children and another on the way.

It's captivating how the lives of the passengers played out in parallel universes over the past 42 years.

Kathy sent me this email dated June 29, 2017

Burt, thanks for your call. My husband and I thoroughly enjoyed our conversation with Captain Eby last week. He seems amazing for 99 years old! We took the opportunity to thank him, of course, and he recounted some details of the flight, most of which I had already read or heard. He also asked me if I thought he should have told us what happened and I assured him that it was best that we didn't know or we may have had trouble getting on the next flight!

I'm attaching a note and photo I emailed to him. I haven't heard back but I hope he received it.

Take care!
Kathy

Dear Captain Eby,

I can't tell you how thrilling it was to speak with you today! I wish I had searched for you years ago to thank you for saving all of us from disaster back in 1975! I've thought of you many times over the years, always grateful that we had a pilot with such skills and experience!

I'm attaching a photo of my family. My husband, Mike, and I have been married 40 years. We have two children and six grandchildren. Our wonderful daughter-in-law is also in the photo but our grandson is away at camp. They all know the story and I asked them to wave to express their appreciation to you.

I'm so thankful that all of our lives were spared back in 1975 and that we were all given many more years to make an impact in the lives of others.

God Bless you, Captain Eby
With much love and appreciation,

Kathy Staff
Carbondale, Illinois.

Staff family

My identical twin daughters, Leslie and Laura, shared their recollections and emotions about flight 182 and our miraculous survival.

From Leslie Sue Herman Resis:

A fraction of a second! It is beyond my comprehension that that is how close I was to death at the young age of 12! I was so excited to be getting on a plane traveling out east to visit relatives for Thanksgiving! With my glass of Coca Cola in one hand, and library book in my other, things couldn't get much better at that moment ... until a few moments later when we experienced some major turbulence, and then absolute chaos! It was a surreal feeling of weightlessness for several seconds followed by everything crashing back down. I thought for sure we hit a humongous air pocket. Thankfully, I had my seat belt on, but several other passengers didn't, and some of them, as well as the flight attendants were injured. I remember watching my dad trying to help one of the flight attendants who was bleeding pretty badly. The airplane was a huge mess with drinks splashed about, food splattered everywhere, and badly injured passengers lying in the aisles. It was beyond frightening! I couldn't believe what I was seeing! I've seen scenes like this in the movies, but this wasn't a movie. This was real life. This was my life!

When we learned the next day about what had actually happened to our airplane, that we came within 20 feet of colliding with another airplane, I couldn't believe it. We were truly able to be thankful on that Thanksgiving Day, and I was going to have an amazing story to share with my friends and classmates when I got back to school.

For several years after the incident, I was afraid to fly. To this day, I'm still terrified of turbulence.

I often think about how lucky I am to be alive, and to have had so many amazing life experiences since that day back in November, 1975 ... My twin sister's and my b'nai mitzvah just six months after the incident, graduations from junior high, high school and college, a career in accounting, amazing friendships, a wonderful marriage, and most importantly, two beautiful daughters, now ages 13 and 17, who are alive today only because of the heroic actions of our pilot, Guy Eby.

From Laura Beth Herman Winter:

Thinking back to Thanksgiving Evening, 1975, and our "near miss" incident over the Michigan skies, I struggle to remember the vast majority of details of that potentially fateful night. However, what I do recall will be forever ingrained in my mind.

I remember sitting next to Mom and Leslie and across the aisle were Dad and Laurence (I think in that order). I recollect enjoying a cold Coca Cola while waiting for dinner to be served. Perhaps I was reading a book or maybe just daydreaming about the family reunion I was looking forward to that weekend.

And then, sheer terror! A sudden steep decent! Our plane went into a nosedive! What?! Did our pilot lose control of the aircraft? Was this it? Like in the movies? I looked around the plane...pure pandemonium! I witnessed beverage and dinner carts racing down the aisles and flight attendants being strewn about. I saw Laurence, who wasn't buckled in, hit his head against the overhead bin. The sensation I felt as we were "falling out of the sky" was familiar; it was like the deepest drop of a roller coaster, only on this ride, there was literally no end in sight.

I screamed and cried in Mom's arms for what seemed like minutes, but was actually only seconds until we finally leveled off and everything and everyone came crashing down. Still petrified and unsure of what just happened, I noticed my favorite blue overalls had just been soaked by my drink and accompanying ice. I don't recall much else while we were on the plane, until we made it safely to the gate. I remember feeling the gravity (no pun intended) of the situation when I observed a few passengers and flight attendants being taken off the plane in stretchers.

I vaguely recall being in the Detroit airport amongst the

crowds, commotion, and confusion. I was just happy to be on the ground. But I soon learned that we would continue on our journey to Newark and I would have to get back on a plane to do so. Talk about being a "white knuckle flyer"! For that flight and many after, the slightest bit of turbulence had me gripping my armrests as if my life depended on it. Over the years, my fear of flying subsided as I came to believe in the expression, lightning doesn't strike twice.

Once we were back home safe and sound, I do recall telling my friends and schoolmates about our incident, which by then we learned was our pilots heroic efforts to avoid a midair collision with an oncoming plane. Needless to say, they were all fascinated, and admittedly, I enjoyed the attention I garnered from sharing the story.

Looking back and reflecting upon our "near miss" in the sky, I think about how lucky we were to have had a skilled pilot save us from what reportedly would have been the worst mid-air collision in modern aviation. Our pilot, Guy Eby, is truly my family's hero. However, I feel that another star is beginning to emerge from this story ... my dad! Through Dad's inspirational speeches and writings over the years, he has been able to reconnect with Guy Eby, and in so doing, has kept this story alive.

We are thrilled that Dad was recently able to finally meet Guy and show our family's appreciation for saving our lives. Dad's recent efforts have given our Thanksgiving miracle story wings that are propelling it to new heights and finally giving Guy Eby the recognition he so deserves!

Three weeks after flight 182, a note was left for Guy at the cockpit door of the DC-10 he had just landed at JFK from LAX. The note, from a flight attendant, was written on the back of a boarding pass a passenger left behind on seat 5 A. She said she couldn't find anything else to write on.

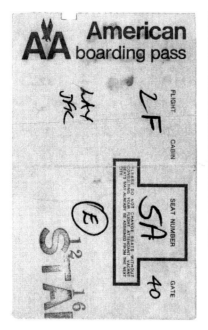 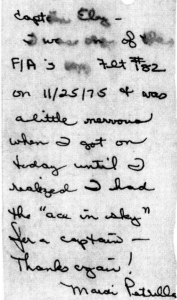

Thoughts from my grandson, Robby Winter:

The world we live in is, in my opinion, just a series of events compounded on top of each other. Once an event takes place, it gets added to the mound of events that have already taken place, and once an event is a part of the mound, it influences all the events that can be added thereafter. As a result of this, the farther back an event goes, the greater and more widespread the impact it has. When Guy Eby saved my family's lives, in the short run, the effects were somewhat small, but as time went on and more and more events piled on the fact that their lives were saved instead of ended, the effects grew drastically. Now, dozens of years later, the consequences are nearly global.

Because I was born, I have affected other people in ways they would not have been if I had not been born, and these people have in turn impacted other people, and so on and so on. As such, to say that we would live in a completely different world had it not been for Guy Eby's fraction-of-a-second reaction time would be an understatement. We would be looking at an entirely different mound and an entirely different set of events in the future.

And how about this letter to the Editor of the *Daytona Beach News-Journal*:

> *In these days of so much negativity and disheartening news throughout the world, it was so encouraging to be reminded of the value of gratitude. I am very proud of the News-Journal for making the story of Guy Eby and Bud Herman a priority. I hope the News-Journal keeps up the good work of balancing tragedy with positive stories as a reminder to feel and express gratitude each day of our lives.*
>
> *C. P. / Holly Hill*

On September 3, 2017, Guy wrote,

I'm amazed at the response of the passengers. Each one has a different story to tell. They are all very appreciative of my quick reaction. You may add my phone number somewhere in the book. Hopefully, it will find more passengers from the flight, as well as the flight attendants.

American Airlines

Guy Eby
Captain, Retired

71 N. St. Andrews Dr.
Ormond Beach, Florida 32074
904-677-1357

TWENTY-EIGHT

The Hero of the
Miracle over Michigan

2017

Hero: "A person who is admired or idealized for
courage, outstanding achievements, or noble qualities."

(Oxford English Dictionary)

Every individual sets their own standards on what constitutes
a hero. For many of us, a hero may simply be an ordinary
individual, a scientist, Doctors Without Borders, a handicapped
person overcoming difficulties and following his or her dreams
finding strength to preserve and endure in spite of the obsta-
cles faced—a search and rescue hurricane first responder or a
member of the military whose sacrifices enabled future generations to have a chance to live in peace and security. Heroes are
everyday civil servants like police officers and firefighters whom
we rely on in times of need and who demur at the mention of
their heroism. And then there's the *Master of The Moment* who
also demurs at the mention of his heroics.

Guy Eby was never at a loss for what to do in an emergency. His passion for knowing how things worked, his curiosity about failure, and his egoless attention to detail in the task before him made him successful. He expected, welcomed, and was fascinated by challenges. Each problem was an opportunity to learn and his confidence grew with his knowledge and wonderment.

Like a bright marble in the hand of a child that flicks toward the circle on the sidewalk and rolls easily and directly to the target, like a ricocheting billiard ball, Guy hit all the angles on his way to the pocket. Like a dancer and athlete, he played with space. Guy was an artist as well as an engineer; he was the Master of the Moment.

When asked about his life and love of aviation, Guy said, "As a child, I never imagined the delicate power flying required or that the experience would be more than a physical, intellectual, and emotional one. More than all that, it is a spiritual experience, flying with the Gods."

AFT

On September 25, 1978, a PSA (Pacific Southwest Airlines) Boeing 727 collided with a Cessna over San Diego's North Park neighborhood, killing 144, making it the deadliest midair disaster in California history.

The flight number was *182*.

On June 23, 1985, an Air India Boeing 747 operating on the Toronto to London to Delhi route was blown out of the sky by a bomb at an altitude of 37,000 feet over the Atlantic while in Irish Air space, killing 329 people.

The flight number was *182*.

And if that isn't eerie enough there were *182* passengers on American Airlines flight *182* Thanksgiving eve 1975.

The great Pythagoras said, "Everything in the universe is mathematically precise; that numbers have special meanings."

I learned that 182 is an angel number with a special meaning for the Herman family.

Herman family

Thanks to the Master of the Moment and the Angels, we were the lucky flight 182. And this is the lucky Herman family. (2017)

Guy's American Airlines captain's hat, the one he wore Thanksgiving eve 1975 is nailed to a wall of his home.

I guess you can say, "He nailed it!"

As of September 7, 2017, I have identified sixteen of the American flight 182 passengers, plus three crew members and Guy heard from a TWA 37 passenger. Hopefully this book will lead to other passengers on both flights.

Thinking about a passenger/crew reunion.

For the passengers and crew of American 182 and TWA 37, November 26, 1975 will always be a profound reminder that every day, every minute and every breath we take is a gift, and each moment of life is a miracle and mystery.

As for moments of life, November 9, 2017 was Guy Eby's 99th birthday. Happy birthday to "The Master of The Moment!"

Guy, may you keep on flying high and making beautiful music for many more years to come.

CBS is planning to do the "Guy Eby Story" on the 43rd anniversary of Flight 182 which will be November 26, 2018. Guy and I have already been interviewed. The story will be aired on Decades TV… "Through the Decades With Bill Kurtis."

THE WHITE HOUSE

WASHINGTON

April 23, 2018

Mr. Guy Eby
Ormond Beach, Florida

Dear Mr. Eby,

I extend my sincere gratitude and respect for your courage and sacrifice as both a Lieutenant in the United States Navy and as a pilot in commercial aviation.

Our Nation owes your generation, the Greatest Generation, a tremendous debt of gratitude for your dedicated service to our country during World War II. In the face of uncertainty and danger, your sacrifices were critical to the defense of our Nation and ensured security and prosperity for millions of people.

It is evident that you carried the Navy's timeless virtues of duty and honor with you to your airline career. Your quick thinking and skill as the pilot of American Airlines Flight 182 prevented a near fatal collision and saved the lives of every passenger on board, many of whom will continue to share your inspiring story with future generations of Americans.

I pray that you are filled with much pride as you reflect on your remarkable legacy as an American hero. May God bless you and your family.

Sincerely,

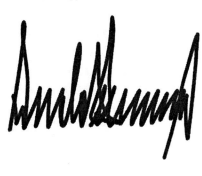

ADDENDUM

Captain's Irregularity Report

Guy Eby's words ②

AA FORM F 27-L
PRINTED IN U.S.

CAPTAIN'S IRREGULARITY REPORT

DATE THIS REPORT __November 26, 1975__

FLIGHT NO. __182__   ORIGINATING STATION __ORD__   DATE ORIGINATED __11/26/75__   AIRCRAFT TYPE __DC-10__   FAA NO. N- __124__

EMERGENCY DECISION [x]	OVERWEIGHT LANDING ☐	ENGINE OUT ☐	DEVIATION FROM REGS ☐	DUMPING FUEL ☐	OTHER [x]

Flight departed __ORD__ at __2339__ GMT **XX**. Irregularity occured at __0024__ GMT **XX**. in vicinity of

__26 mi. W. CRL__ _____ while taking off _____ climbing __35000__ cruising _____

descending ⑧ _____ landing _____ Altitude __35000__ Flight landed __DTW__ at __0050__ ST.

WEATHER – VFR or INST? If INST, give actual weather. **In clouds stars above.**

~~I was the Captain of AAL Flt. 182 on Nov. 26, 1975.~~ While on CLE ARTCC frequency we were cleared to FL 330. Before reaching FL330 we were recleared to climb to FL370. Approaching or going throu FL350 we were instructed to "descend immediately to FL330". I immediately started descent with the auto-pilot vertical speed control. Simultaneously I sighted another aircraft at 12 o'clock opposite direction. I manually increased nose down and then further increased forward pressure to avoid the other aircraft. From sighting to passing of the other aircraft overhead, estimated time 3 to 4 seconds. Estimated distance between aircraft at passing, 100 feet vertically.

At time of incident (1924E) we were in IFR conditions. During climb intermittent choppy air was encountered and seat belt sign was on during entire flight. Upon reaching FL330 I was informed of cabin injuries. I instructed the First Officer to request landing at DTW. I then instructed the Flight Engineer to pull the Voice Recorder circuit breaker. He informed me that the voice recorder circuit breaker was pulled and that he had activated the Event Button on the Flight Recorder. Duri descent to DTW I instructed the Flight Engineer to inform the Company of injuries on board and to have medical assistance and ambulances standing by to meet the flight. Descent was executed as quickly as possible in accordance with ATC instructions.

During descent a PA was made informing the passengers that a landing would be made at DTW. The cabin crew was informed that a normal landing would be made in DTW. My decision to land at DTW was to provide medical assistance to injured passengers and crew.

Engine failure or stoppage was reported at_____ ST. to ARINC Station At_____ . Complete information on back for type of equipment on which the failure or stoppage occurred.

Airplane was landed approximately _____ lbs. overweight. Dumped _____ lbs. fuel.

The above action was taken in accordance with FAR and, for the reason given, was considered to be the best procedure to effect the safe conduct of the flight.

Captain _[signature]_   Base __JFK__

I have reviewed the above and (concur) do not concur / with the action taken by the Captain.

Manager Flying / Base Supt. Flying / Flying Instruction Director _[signature]_ Date __12/1/75__
D. A. Wetherbee FR

I concur with the action taken by the Captain.

Asst. Vice President Flying _____ Date_____

Vice Pres. Flying Training _____ Date_____

APA Accident Investigation Commission 11/29/75

Nov. 29, 1975

Capt. Harold R. Miller
Chairman, Central Safety Comm.
Allied Pilots Association
Arlington, Texas

Dear Harold:

As you may know, I attended the NTSB Hearing regarding Flight 182 of November 26th, held at LGA on November 27th. Capt. Harvey Wenz also represented APA. He and I reached generally the same conclusions.

CREW: Capt. Guy Eby
       F/O   David Narins
       F/E   Bruce Hopkins

POSITION: Approx. 25DME West of CRL VOR

WEATHER: IFR, In the tops-very limited foward visibility.

Incident: All three crewmembers gave basically the same tes-
           timony. The flight was cleared by Cleveland ATC
           to FL 370, before reaching FL 330 they were re-
           cleared to maintain 330, and then again cleared
           to FL 370. As they passed through about FL 345-348
           they were told to descend immdeiately to FL 330.
           During the gradual pitch over from climb to descent,
           " the windscreen filled with airplane." Capt. Eby
           pushed the yoke foward, while disengaging the auto-
           pilot, in order to avoid the other aircraft. Negative
           "G" resulted, and the aircraft was leveled at FL330.
               The maneuver resulted in injuries in the cabin
           and Capt. Eby elected to land at DTW. The subsequent
           landing was uneventful.

Conclusion: A near miss was avoided by prompt crew action.

Cabin Problems: It is very interestin to see what resulted
           in the cabin as a result of the negative "g" loading
           and subsequent return to positive "g". A number of
           Flight Attendants were injured and also, a number
           of passengers, none of whom had their seat belts
           fastened. (The seat belt sign was on.) The service
           carts that were in the ailses and the FA's were thrown
           through the ceiling trim and then back to the floor,
           somewhat the worse for wear. The FA's testified that
           the carts came completely apart throwing their con-
           tents, drawers, partions etc. about the aircraft and
           causing injury.
               The FA's with the help of a deadheading cabin
           crew were able to clean up the aircraft and restow
           ceiling panels that had fallen prior to landing in
           the event that an evacuation might be required.

Opinion: Capt. Wenz and I both feel that the carts in the
           ailses are a hazard and the method of their use requires
           study.

Cockpit Voice Recorder

NATIONAL TRANSPORTATION SAFETY BOARD
Bureau of Aviation Safety
Washington, D. C.

SPECIALIST'S FACTUAL REPORT OF INVESTIGATION
COCKPIT VOICE RECORDER

BY

Paul C. Turner
Aerospace Engineer

Warning

The reader of this report is cautioned that the transcription
of a CVR tape is not a precise science but is the best product
possible from an NTSB group investigative effort. The transcript
or parts thereof, if taken out of context, could be misleading.
The attached CVR transcript should be viewed as an accident investigation tool to be used in conjunction with other evidence gathered
during the investigation. Conclusions or interpretations should not
be made using the transcript as the sole source of information.

NATIONAL TRANSPORTATION SAFETY BOARD
Bureau of Aviation Safety
Washington, D. C.

December 19, 1975

SPECIALIST'S FACTUAL REPORT OF INVESTIGATION
COCKPIT VOICE RECORDER

A. ACCIDENT

Location: Detroit, Illinois
Date   : November 26, 1975
Operator: American Airlines and Trans World Airlines
Aircraft: Douglas DC-10 vs. Lockheed L-1011
CVR   : American-Fairchild A-100, S/N 3084
NTSB No.: DCA 76-A-Z012

B. GROUP

Paul Turner, National Transportation Safety Board, Chairman
Guy Eby, American Airlines, Member
Ivan Reddington, Allied Pilots Association, Member
Ross Morse, Allied Pilots Association, Member
Jay H. Theder, Allied Pilots Association, Member
Frank Lamm, American Airlines, Member

C. SUMMARY OF INVESTIGATION

The cockpit voice recorder from the above accident aircraft
was brought to the NTSB Audio Lab where a routine transcript was
prepared with the aid of crewmembers. A 1-percent timing error
may exist.

Paul C. Turner
Aerospace Engineer

Attachment

TRANSCRIPT OF AN AMERICAN AIRLINES AIRCRAFT WITH A FAIRCHILD
CVR S/N 3084 WHICH HAD A NEAR MISS WITH A TRANS WORLD AIRLINES
AIRCRAFT NEAR DETROIT, ILLINOIS, NOVEMBER 26, 1975

LEGEND

CAM	Cockpit area microphone voice or sound source
RDO	Radio transmission or PA from aircraft AA182
-1	Voice identified as Captain
-2	Voice identified as First Officer
-3	Voice identified as Second Officer
-?	Voice unidentified
UNK	Unknown
CHIC	Chicago Center
CLEC	Cleveland Center
75LE	An aircraft
AA26	An American aircraft
U374	A United aircraft
T61	A TWA aircraft
U680	A United aircraft
T37	A TWA aircraft
*	Unintelligible word
#	Nonpertinent word
%	Break in continuity
( )	Questionable text
(( ))	Editorial insertion
---	Pause

Note: Times are in elapsed time (minutes and seconds).

- 2 -

TIME & SOURCE	CONTENT

00:00
CHIC

American one eighty-two, maintain flight level three seven zero

00:05
RDO-2

One eight-two is out of two seven point nine for three seven oh

00:10
CHIC

One eighty-two have you roger direct Carlton on course contact Cleveland Center one two seven point zero five

00:15
RDO-2

One twenty-seven oh five and its direct Carl--, ah, Carlton on course, so long

00:21
CHIC

Bye now, nine twenty-two contact --- %

00:30
RDO-2

Cleveland Center, American's flight one eighty-two heavy with you out of two eight oh for three seven zero

00:35
CLEC

American one eighty-two, roger, squawk three two zero two and ident --- and ah seven five lima echo that heading looks good for London

00:45
75LE

Okay we'll maintain zero eight five

00:55
AA26

American twenty-six level, three seven zero

01:01
CHIC

American twenty-six, roger

01:31
CAM-2

The stars are beginning to dimly appear

CAM-1

Yes

CAM-2

But dimly

03:15
CHIC

United three seventy-four, Cleveland one three four ah one one eight six five one eighteen sixty-five United three seventy-four

- 3 -

TIME & SOURCE	CONTENT

03:27
CHIC
United three seventy-four Cleveland do you copy?

03:31
U374
Ah, go ahead, please

03:33
CLEC
United three seventy-four, Cleveland one one eight six five, one eighteen sixty-five

03:38
U374
Roger

04:46
T61
TWA sixty-one with ya level three five oh, light chop

05:26
T61
Cleveland TWA six one level at three five oh

05:30
CHIC
TWA, sixty one roger

05:59
U680
Good evening Cleveland Center, United six eighty's out of twenty-eight five for three three oh, which will do for final

06:06
CLEC
Six eighty, Cleveland Center roger maintain flight level three three zero

06:10
U680
Okay --- any idea of the tops

06:15
CLEC
No, they were at thirty-five earlier just a minute let me check

06:19
CLEC
TWA thirty-seven Cleveland what are the tops?

06:22
T37
Ah, higher than we are, ah, it's hard to say, you can see through it, but ah I'd say it must be at least three seven

148

- 4 -

| TIME & SOURCE | CONTENT |

06:31
CLEC Okay TWA thirty-seven, thank you

06:35
CLEC Six eight did you copy?

06:37
U680 Yeah, thank you

06:45
A26 American twenty-six is just skimming the tops

06:50
CLEC Okay American twenty-six, thank you and United six eighty that aircraft's at three seven oh

06:55
U680 Okay

06:59
CLEC American one eighty-two Cleveland, what is your altitude?

07:03
RDO-2 Passing through three four point seven at this time, we can see stars above us but we're still in the area of the clouds

07:12

07:11
CAM-1 ~~There he is~~ *where he is*

07:12
CLEC *AMERICAN* One eight two descend immediately to three three oh *Clev Contr*
07:14

07:14
RDO-2 Descending to three three oh at this time *First Officer*
16

07:17
CAM-2 There he is - *first officer*

07:18
CAM-2/3 # what kind of game is this! *first off*
 2nd off

07:19
CLEC TWA seventy-seven traffic ((sound similar to objects being thrown about starts and continues for about two seconds))

TIME & SOURCE	CONTENT

07:21
CAM   ((Sound of objects being thrown about the cockpit: occurs beginning with the word "game" and continues for about two seconds))

07:26
CAM-3   * we missed *2nd officer*

07:27
CAM-1   Huh! *Captain*

07:28
CAM-2   # *1st officer*

07:32
CAM   ((Mach overspeed warning comes on and continues for 18 seconds))

07:43
CAM-1   What altitude were we at? *Captain*

07:47
CAM-1   * * *Cap.*

07:52
RDO-2   American one eight-two is at three three oh *1st officer*

07:56
CLEC   One eighty-two, thank you *Controller*

07:58
CAM-2   # #

08:00
CAM-2   Shall I say anything to them? *1st officer*

08:02
CAM-1   Ask 'em what altitude that other aircraft was at *Captain*

08:03
RDO-2   What altitude was that other aircraft at?

08:06
CLEC   Thirty-five sir

- 6 -

TIME & SOURCE	CONTENT

08:08
CAM-1   Good Gosh!

08:09
CAM-2   (He was) not at thirty-five

08:11
CAM-3   Yeah (he) might of been

08:12
RDO-2   I'd check on that

08:13
CLEC   * will do

08:16
CAM-3   (Okay), we got trouble in the back, that's for sure

08:17
CAM-1   * *

08:20
CAM-3   Hello -- okay

02:23
CAM-3   Captain, somebody's desparately hurt back there

08:26
CAM-1   Huh?

08:27
CAM-3   We have people desperately hurt back there

08:28
CAM-1   I think we better put into Detroit

08:32
CAM-3   Captain, I can't hear what you said

08:34
CAM-1   I think we better go into Detroit

08:35
CAM-3   All right

08:46
RDO-2   Okay American's one eighty-two's at three three zero request routing to Detroit

TIME & SOURCE	CONTENT
08:57 CLEC	American one eight-two, Cleveland Center, roger, understand you want to land at Detroit now?
09:01 RDO-2	That's affirmative
09:04 CLEC	One eighty-two Cleveland Center, standby one
09:16 CLEC	American one eighty-two Cleveland descend to flight level two four zero, fly heading of two six --- correction make it zero six zero
09:23 RDO-2	Going to two four
09:24 CAM	((Cockpit conversation concerning the preparation for an approach and landing at Detroit))
	((End of Recording))

Analysis and Conclusion

TECHNICAL REPORT DOCUMENTATION PAGE

1. Report No. NTSB-AAR-76-3	2. Government Accession No.	3. Recipient's Catalog No.
4. Title and Subtitle Aircraft Accident Report - Near Collision, American Airlines, Inc., Douglas DC-10, N124 and Trans World Airlines, Inc., Lockheed 1011, N11002, Near Carleton, Michigan, November 26, 1975		5. Report Date January 28, 1976
		6. Performing Organization Code
7. Author(s)		8. Performing Organization Report No.
9. Performing Organization Name and Address National Transportation Safety Board Bureau of Aviation Safety Washington, D.C. 20594		10. Work Unit No. 1736
		11. Contract or Grant No.
12. Sponsoring Agency Name and Address NATIONAL TRANSPORTATION SAFETY BOARD Washington, D. C. 20594		13. Type of Report and Period Covered Aircraft Accident Report November 26, 1975
		14. Sponsoring Agency Code

15. Supplementary Notes

16. Abstract

On November 26, 1975, American Airlines Douglas DC-10 and a Trans World Airlines Lockheed-1011 almost collided head-on at 35,000 feet near Carleton, Michigan. Both aircraft were operating in instrument meteorological conditions, within positive control airspace, and while under the control of the Cleveland Air Route Traffic Control Center. As a result of the evasive maneuver executed by the captain of the DC-10, 3 aircraft occupants were injured seriously and 21 were injured slightly. The cabin's interior was damaged extensively. None of the occupants of the L-1011 was injured.

The National Transportation Safety Board determines that the probable cause of this near-collision was the failure of the radar controller to apply prescribed separation criteria when he first became aware of a potential traffic conflict which necessitated an abrupt collision avoidance maneuver. He also allowed secondary duties to interfere with the timely detection of the impending traffic conflict when it was displayed clearly on his radarscope. Contributing to the accident was an incomplete sector briefing during the change of controller personnel--about 1 minute before the accident.

17. Key Words Air traffic control, positive control airspace, distraction of attention, evasive maneuver, near-collision	18. Distribution Statement This document is available to the public through the National Technical Information Service, Springfield, Virginia 22191
19. Security Classification (of this report) UNCLASSIFIED	20. Security Classification (of this page) UNCLASSIFIED	21. No. of Pages 21	22. Price

NTSB Form 1765.2 (Rev. 9/74)

Crew and Controller Information

APPENDIX B

CREW AND CONTROLLER INFORMATION

Captain Guy Eby (American Airlines)

Captain Eby, 57, holds Airline Transport Pilot Certificate No. 261304 with type ratings in DC-3,6,7,10, L-188, CV-240,340,440,880,990 and B-707,720. At the time of the accident he had accumulated about 21,600 flight-hours, 670 of which had been in the DC-10. His last proficiency check in the DC-10 was completed satisfactorily on June 30, 1975. He possessed a current first-class medical certificate dated October 7, 1975, with no limitations.

First Officer David Narins (American Airlines)

First Officer Narins, 43, holds Airline Transport Pilot Certificate No. 1447244 with type ratings in B-707, B-720, and DC-3. At the time of the accident he had accumulated about 7,500 flight-hours, about 300 hours of which had been in the DC-10. His last proficiency check in the DC-10 was completed satisfactorily on July 16, 1975. He possessed a current second-class medical certificate, dated December 30, 1974, with no limitations.

Flight Engineer Bruce A. Hopkins (American Airlines)

Flight Engineer Hopkins, 53, holds Flight Engineer Certificate No. 718201. At the time of the accident, he had accumulated about 22,350 flight-hours, about 1,450 of which had been in the DC-10. His last check in the DC-10 was completed satisfactorily on June 11, 1975. He possessed a current second-class medical certificate, dated June 3, 1975, with no limitations.

Flight Attendants

The 10 flight attendants were qualified.

Air Traffic Control Specialist Drew Parker (Radar Controller)

ATC Specialist Parker, 31, holds an Air Traffic Control Certificate and a second-class medical certificate without limitations. He has served as an air traffic controller in the United States Air Force (USAF) for 4 years. He has been employed by the FAA for about 7 years and has been a fully qualified journeyman controller at Cleveland Center for 4 years. He has no aviation experience as a pilot or other crewmember.

The circumstances of this accident indicate that automation technology can lead to complacency when it takes the controller "out of the loop" by reducing the need for his interaction with a flightcrew and deemphasizing the cooperative aspects of the air traffic system. Had the radar controller been working with the broad-band radar, he would have 'been forced to take positive steps to insure separation as soon as American 182 was handed off to him. Of the several steps he could have taken, we mention only two: (1) He could have stopped American 182's climb at FL 330, or (2) he could have asked the flight to report at FL 310 or 330. However, the automatic altitude readouts on the flight's alpha-numeric block induced him to rely solely on his own observation of the PVD data. He did not consider the possibility that he might become distracted or that the computer might fail, and thereby deprive him of his direct readout capability.

The Safety Board is concerned that despite the advantages of narrow-band radar, the ATC system failed to provide the intended safeguard and endangered the lives of 306 persons'. Advances in technology do not necessarily insure greater reliability and safety. The new conflict-alert system can serve its intended purpose only when it is not treated as' a substitute for timely, positive separation measures which continue to protect air traffic even when the computer fails.

Based on the high percentage of human failures in the ATC system, the Safety Board believes that, as long as the human element is part of the total system, an individual's level of competence, the quality of his performance, and his understanding of his primary responsibilities must be given as much managerial attention as the equipment he operates.

The serious injuries sustained by the passengers were the result of their not having their seatbelts fastened, or properly fastened, although the seatbelt sign was on. Therefore, this accident is another reminder to encourage passengers to keep their seatbelts fastened, not only when the seatbelt sign is on but also when it is off and flight conditions are smooth.

Conclusions

(a) Findings

1. American 182 and TWA 37 were operating under control of the Wayne sector of the Cleveland Center.

2. Both flights were on the same jet route and approaching each other head-on; TWA 37 was maintaining FL 350, American 182 was cleared to climb through FL 350 to FL 370.

3. The radar controller was aware that a potential traffic conflict existed between the two flights but assumed that the required separation would exist when the two aircraft passed each other.

4. The radar controller intended to provide separation if the anticipated separation between the two flights did not materialize.

5. The radar controller became preoccupied with secondary duties and failed to see the impending traffic conflict displayed on his radarscope.

6. About 1 minute before the near collision, the radar controller was relieved and he failed to brief the relieving controller adequately. Both controllers failed to notice the unresolved conflict during the transfer of duties.

7. About 50 seconds after taking over the position, the second controller detected the conflict and cleared American 182 to descend immediately to FL 330.

8. The two aircraft came within 100 feet of each other.

9. As a result of the abrupt evasive maneuver, 24 occupants of the aircraft were injured, 3 of them seriously; the latter injuries were associated with failure to make proper use of the seatbelt.

(b) Probable Cause

The National Transportation Safety Board determines that the probable cause of this near-collision was the failure of the radar controller to apply prescribed separation criteria when he first became aware of a potential traffic conflict, which necessitated an abrupt collision avoidance maneuver. He also allowed secondary duties to interfere with the timely detection of the impending traffic conflict when it was displayed clearly on his radarscope. Contributing to the accident was an incomplete sector briefing during the change of controller personnel--about 1 minute before the accident.

156

WWII Combat Report

The following article is a nearly-verbatim official report of PBM seaplane combat action in the Pacific during WWII. Wings of Gold thanks former AOMIC of Crew Two, Jack Christopher of VPB-27, for his assistance with this story.

3 July 1945 Two PBMs on an anti-shiping search were heading 130 degrees just off the Yangtze Cape at 31-00N, 122-00E shortly before noon when three Japanese fighters (Ki-44s; *code name, Tojos*) attacked out of the sun. LT R. S. Scott was flying the lead PBM with LTJG W.H. Dompier in the right seat when another Japanese fighter made a head-on approach from 3,000 feet toward the PBMs at 1,500 feet with the second plane a mile behind the first. AS LT Scott saw the enemy aircraft come down out of the sun, he added power and nosed over to get down close to the water. Within 20 seconds, however, the enemy plane had closed, opened up with what may have been 40mm fire and severely damaged the PBM, wounding both pilots and two crewmen. One explosive shell hit just aft of the bow turret and exploded against the instrument panel. This

PBM Mariner. (Rich Dann Collection)

shell severely wounded the pilot about the legs, body and face, rendering him unconscious. The copilot received a severe facial wound and blood flowing from the gash blinded him.

LTJG Guy Eby, the navigator, was near the flight engineer's panel when the shell hit. He ran forward and as the plane was still in a steep glide with full power and full RPM, Eby grabbed the yoke from the dazed copilot, and attempted to pull the plane up. But the nose-up elevator control had been shot away and the plane failed to respond. Eby immediately rolled nose-up tab and succeeded in pulling the plane up when it was less than 300 feet from the water and was indicating better than 200 knots.

With the plane heading upward, LTJG Eby helped LT Dompier from the right seat and took over the controls, finally getting the plane squared away in level flight. After a few minutes, when a fire in the bow had been extinguished, LTJG Eby called the plane captain and others, who removed LT Scott from the left seat and took him to a bunk aft where they provided emergency treatment. To get away from the shore line, LTJG Eby changed course to 060 degrees.

Meanwhile, the second PBM, piloted by ENS Hans K. Kohler, which was flying about a mile astern, was bearing the brunt of subsequent attacks levied by the three Tojos. Of the attacks on ENS Kohler however, only one was aggressive. The first attack on ENS Kohler's plane came when he had descended to about 1,800 feet, following astern LT Scott. When the first fighter attacked the lead plane, ENS Kohler turned into it as the Tojo broke away to the left of LT Scott's PBM. ENS Kohler's bow gunner fired 50 to 100 rounds into the departing enemy fighter, and crew members thought some of the hits went home. As ENS Kohler turned back to a course of 60 degrees to follow the lead plane, one fighter made a pass from the port beam. ENS Kohler turned into him and although the PBM was only 50 to 75 feet off the water, the fighter passed beneath (the PBM). Kohler jettisoned his remaining bombs and continued on course as another enemy plane came in from the starboard side just forward of the beam. Kohler continued on course with all his guns firing at the approaching plane. The fighter, seeing tracers headed his way, broke off the attack before he had closed to effective range. ENS Kohler's gunners reported that all shots from the fighter fell short, hitting the water beneath..

A few seconds later, another Japanese plane made a stern attack, but this was not aggressive and the Tojo pulled away after the tail gunner had fired only a few bursts from his turret. The planes continued on course with enemy fighters paralleling their track for nearly 15 minutes.

Next, the three fighters headed back to their base in China. A summary of the attacks shows that only one run was made on LT Scott's PBM, but this was plenty aggressive and resulted in a total of four 40mm hits on the PBM, and minor damage from five to six .25 caliber holes. ENS Kohler had three runs made on his aircraft but these were not aggressive and the PBM sustained no damage.

A summary of the damage to LT Scott's plane shows that one 20mm explosive shell exploded against the instrument panel destroying all instruments in the pilot's seat and wounding both pilots. Another exploded in the starboard wing just inboard of the engine, making several holes in the wing tank.

Two other explosive shells hit the tail assembly. One struck the vertical stabilizer on the starboard side, the other in the left vertical stabilizer. So much for the exciting action of the day.

(Note: the following describes previous action that day.)

Before meeting the fighters, the two prowling PBMs attacked a tug in a small cove at 31-20N, 121-52E. Both planes made a coordinated attack with LT Scott strafing and dropping one string of bombs (three 100-pounders and one fire bomb) and ENS Kohler strafing. The bomb drop appeared to be a perfect straddle and the target was probably sunk. This action occurred at 1043.

At 1105 at 31-15N, 121-45E the PBMs spotted targets, a tug which was towing a barge, with a Sugar Dog (nomenclature for a trawler used at the time) which was cruising along the port side of the barge about one-half mile distance. LT Scott went in on a strafing run and ENS Kohler followed with a strafing run and dropped a string of bombs (three 100 pounders and one fire bomb). The bomb drop blanketed the tug and left it sinking and burning. One bomb was a direct hit.

As the two planes came around for a second run on the targets, the barge started throwing up AA fire which consisted of parachute bombs. The shells (launched) from the barge would explode at about six to seven hundred feet. A white parachute opened with a cylindrical dark object drifting down beneath it. About a dozen of these objects were thrown up over the target so the PBMs knocked off the attack. However, the tug was left burning and sinking, and the barge was dead in the water.

(Note: during WWII parachute bombs were also dropped by

enemy aircraft on allied planes flying below them.)

On the initial run over the target, the planes came in very low (50-75 feet). The planes had abandoned this target and were looking for others when the fighters jumped them.

5 July 1945 LTs E.A. McQuillan and O.B. Miller, flying a search mission off the China coast, spotted a coastal trawler of about 200 tons in the Saddle Island group shortly after noon. A coordinated bombing and strafing attack was launched by the two Mariners and direct hits were scored by both planes. The ship blew up and sank.

According to Jack Christopher, few stories of the Martin-built PBMs seem to have been published. The PBY Black Cats were well known, of course. PBYs replaced the PBM in combat the last couple of years of the war. The PBMs were heavily armed, including bomb bays in each engine nacelle, it had a great radar that could "see" 120 miles in all directions.

PBMs did a lot. One squadron, VPB-18, with 15 PBMs, sank 34 enemy ships, damaged 28, bombed 24 shore installations, shot down 12 enemy planes, damaged nine others, and rescued 20 pilots.

Jack Christopher, right, with Jim McDougall, at the Flying Cloud airport expo in Minneapolis, MN in July 2015

In Okinawa waters, April 1945, a PBM with Crew 2 of VPB-27 taxies out for an ASW mission. Barely visible in the open hatch forward is former crewmember, Jack Christopher.

CPSIA information can be obtained
at www.ICGtesting.com
Printed in the USA
LVOW11*1732180618
580266LV00001BA/2/P